Leadership for Change

Leadership for Change: A Guide for the Frustrated Nurse

Dorothy A. Brooten
Assistant Professor
School of Nursing
University of Pennsylvania
Philadelphia, Pa.

Laura Lucia Hayman
Associate
School of Nursing
University of Pennsylvania
Philadelphia, Pa.

Mary Duffin Naylor
Assistant Professor
Department of Baccalaureate Nursing
College of Allied Health Sciences
Thomas Jefferson University
Philadelphia, Pa.

J. B. LIPPINCOTT COMPANY

PHILADELPHIA   NEW YORK   SAN JOSE   TORONTO

Copyright © 1978 by J. B. Lippincott Company

Distributed in Great Britain by
Blackwell Scientific Publications
London   Oxford   Edinburgh

ISBN 0-397-54218-6

Library of Congress Catalog Card Number 78-8661

Printed in the United States of America

2 4 6 8 9 7 5 3 1

Library of Congress Cataloging in Publication Data

Brooten, Dorothy A
    Leadership for change.

    Bibliography: p.
    Includes index.
    1. Nursing—Social aspects.   2. Social change.
3. Leadership.   4. Nursing—Political aspects—
United States.   I. Naylor, Mary Duffin, joint author.
II. Hayman, Laura Lucia, joint author.   III. Title.
[DNLM: 1. Education, Nursing—United States.
2. Leadership—Nursing texts.   3. Nursing care.
WY87 B873L]
RT86.5.B75   610.73'0692   78-8661
ISBN 0-397-54218-6

Preface

Why a whole book, even a modest one, about change in nursing? The authors start from a simple set of premises. In order to realize the full potential of nurses to make unique and valuable contributions to effective and humane systems of health care, the nursing profession must heighten its capacity for leadership. That leadersip must be exercised not only within the profession itself, but also in the total health care field and indeed in society at large. One of the increasingly critical skills needed for leadership is a capability to understand and manage the forces that generate change. The most effective leader is one who commands both a theoretical grasp and practical skills for planning and directing change.

These ideas today are hardly revolutionary in nursing. The National League for Nursing has made leadership preparation a basic criterion for evaluating and accrediting professional nursing curricula. Leadership texts increasingly include chapters treating the theory of change. And there is a growing body of literature focusing on change skills as a critical element in determining nurses' influence over issues that vitally affect their ability to deliver professional nursing services effectively. These issues include the financing of health care generally and of nursing care in particular; the organization of health care teams; the scope and standards of professional nursing practice; health maintenance service as opposed to simple management of illness; and the very structure of our emerging future system of health care.

Nurses want to use their unique education and skills more effectively for people, both in illness and in health. This was substantiated by hundreds of responses to the authors' own survey of 1,100 nurses working in a variety of settings across the United States. The survey results found in the appendix helped guide the direction of portions of this book and only served to underscore once again nurses' frustrations with problems in the current system of health care delivery.

Against this background, a work which embraces both the theory and practice of change has a vital role in schools of nursing in both graduate and undergraduate courses dealing with nursing professionalism, socialization, leadership or change theory. It likewise has a vital role in management and staff-level inservice training, continuing education programs for nurses, and as a background reference for nurse educators. This book will also serve as an essential manual for those frustrated graduate nurses who are seriously working to effect change in their practice settings or, through their organizations, in the larger health care system.

Our unique objectives in this book are to unfold in logical sequence a sense of the history of change in nursing, a sense of direction for future change, a theoretical framework and a set of practical guidelines for planning and managing change. The book is offered as a statement of the possible. We write from a firm conviction that the nursing profession can much more effectively influence change around it. In so doing it will both enhance its stature and accomplishment as a profession and shape a better system of health care for our society.

Acknowledgments

We would like to thank many individuals for their support and encouragement in our efforts to complete the manuscript. We must begin by thanking Mr. David Miller, managing editor of the nursing department, for his enthusiasm and support for our project.

Our thanks to Dr. Clifford Jordan, well-known nurse, for his critical review and suggestions for Chapters One and Two. His encouragement at a crucial time in the book's development will always be appreciated. We wish to thank Mrs. Margaret Aiken, a director of diploma nursing education for many years, for her review and suggestions for Chapters One and Two. Thanks are extended to Diane Fescina, a director of inservice education, and Pamela Cioffari, a head nurse, for their review and reactions to the same chapters. We also wish to thank fellow educators Gail Tobey and Dorothy Fischer for their critical review and suggestions.

Our appreciation is extended to Judy Davis, RN, for painstakingly collating the data from the survey questionnaires. We are very grateful to Sharon Limaye, RN, who spent many late evening and early morning hours typing in a final effort to help us meet our manuscript deadline. We would also like to thank all of the nurses who took the time and effort to respond to our survey questionnaire.

We are especially grateful to Gary Brooten for his probing questions and his many substantive and editorial suggestions throughout the history of the project. We also wish to thank him for giving freely of his special expertise in the areas of public relations and legislation.

Rarely are authors able to complete a project without the unending patience and loving support of those most dear to them. This project was no exception. In this regard, loving appreciation is extended to Thomas Naylor and Richard Hayman from their wives.

Contents

ONE

We've Already Done Some

INDIVIDUALS EFFECTING CHANGE

Florence Nightingale began it.
Margaret Sanger carried it on.
Lucille Kinlein continues it.

These individuals have been standouts among nurses who have recognized the need for change, who have had faith in their goals, a grasp of how changes can be made to happen, and courage to act.

They are not alone. Other nurses have acted, too. In ways great and small they have pushed, planned, persisted—and ultimately proved that they *could* change their profession, their working environment, and the quality of health care.

They have been the leaders for change in nursing.

Their names could be strung out over pages. Some have wrought change on a grand scale—Nightingale, Sanger, Wald. Some have stirred change with dramatic breaks from "business as usual"— Breckenridge, Kinlein. Some have founded organizations in which nurses could work together for change—Robb, Nutting, Dock. Beyond the familiar names are untold others whose arenas may have been as modest as a single hospital unit, but whose leadership has had a telling impact within those arenas.

What has made these nurses so special? In at least two ways they have been very much like great numbers of nurses today—keenly aware of urgent needs for change and deeply frustrated by the difficulties of making changes happen.

1

As we look carefully at several of these leaders, we find personal styles as varied as the individuals themselves. We also find common themes in their varied approaches to change—the same themes that appear in the successful change efforts of other nurses.

There are in fact distinct pathways to change in modern society. Some leaders have followed these pathways by instinct, some by inspiration, some by imitating the styles of earlier leaders. By using their examples and new insights of social science, today's nurses can learn practical skills to help them bring about the changes they see needed all around them.

Nightingale as a Leader for Change

Florence Nightingale was the first great leader for change in nursing; many agree the most important. She was a woman with a strong need to do something useful with her life. As a child she had enjoyed nursing animals, and, later, members of her family and peasants in nearby cottages. She also was deeply moved by the poverty and suffering she saw in the villages. These feelings drew her to nursing. But the attitudes of the Victorian era limited the expectations of young women of the privileged classes—they could marry, raise children and arrange social activities for their families, or live out their quiet spinsterhood within the confines of their family estates. No other choices were truly acceptable. For this reason the impulses which were to steer Florence Nightingale to leadership in nursing actually began by placing her in direct, painful conflict with her family and her social circle.

Florence—"Flo" to all who knew her—was born in 1820. Her parents were wealthy and well connected, and provided her with an environment which offered luxury, travel, prestige, education and security. The family divided its time between two very beautiful family estates—summers at Lea Hurst, the ancestral estate in the wild northern countryside, and winters at Embley, in the rich green meadows of southern England. There were frequent visits to gracious homes and estates of relatives. There was travel, often to distant parts of the world. Florence's family entertained and cultivated the friendship of prominent members of the English upper class, and also of celebrated literary, artistic and political figures. Her father himself held political office for a time.

Florence was well educated in classical studies, and was exposed to divergent points of view on many subjects through the steady stream of visitors to the family estates. It was this exposure, as well as her education and experiences, that gave her a very broad perspective, which was heightened by two very special influences. Instead of devoting long hours to learning the traditional activities of women, she preferred to spend long hours in serious discussion of politics and world events with her father. At times she was her father's constant companion. While he was interested in politics as a matter of theory, she was interested in the practical application to the everyday lives of people. His sometimes unorthodox political views also placed him in contact with groups that in other countries would have been considered the radical underground. Young Florence met these people, learned their causes, and often wished that she could be part of them.

The other special influence was her Aunt Julia, Florence's favorite aunt. Aunt Julia was deeply involved in the feminist movement, supporting both the cause and its leaders. She also regularly visited and nursed the poor in nearby villages, often accompanied by young Florence.

So here was the young Miss Nightingale—intelligent, articulate, attractive, polished, secure in a wealthy family. She had everything an ordinary young woman could have wanted in that era, yet she was keenly aware of what other things might be possible for her outside the traditional gentlewoman's role. As she saw it, of what use was all the knowledge she had accumulated? What good would it do anyone—all the studying, all the ideas she had gleaned from her family's visitors and from her travels? She did not wish to limit herself to marrying and arranging social activities. She needed something more.

Nursing represented an avenue by which she could make a contribution to society much like the contributions of the successful people passing through her family's drawing rooms. There was so much to be done in this area, so much to be learned! In it, Florence found promise of satisfactions that had meaning for her.

Her family disagreed. Her parents, her sister, other members of her family and her friends argued vehemently against her idea. It took Florence more than ten years of hard work and study—sometimes in secret—much soul-searching, and even periods of deep depression and suicidal thoughts, before she was able at last to break decisively with her family's expectations and to embark openly on her nursing career.

Florence had prepared herself well for the separation. For several years she had studied hospital design and nursing at every opportunity. At home she rose with the sun, well before anyone else in the family, to study. Her travels also provided her with learning opportunities. After many long months of pleading with her parents, Florence finally got their consent to study at Kaiserwerth with Theodore Fliedner, provided her study was hidden from other members of the family. To them, she would be traveling abroad. She also visited many other hospitals and charitable institutions to study their design, organization and services.

Finally, Florence made the break with her family by assuming the position of Lady Superintendent of the Establishment for the Care of Gentlewomen in Sickness in London. She was supported in her decision by several family friends and some relatives. Eventually her family also would come to accept her new role. Meanwhile, the torment she had experienced during this period was to make later attempts at change more bearable.

Florence did well in her first job. She was soon recognized as an excellent manager and as an expert in hospital design. She conversed and corresponded with leaders in the medical field and through her family maintained ties with leading political figures. She had just begun to consider a more demanding position as superintendent of a large London hospital when world events gave her an even greater opportunity to accomplish significant changes in both nursing and health care delivery.

It was late 1854. England was at war in the Crimea, and the London press was filled with dramatic accounts of the poor medical care and total lack of nursing care for the British troops in battle. The stories contrasted the plight of the British soldiers with the circumstances of the French, who were receiving nursing care from religious orders. After several particularly gruesome stories, the public became outraged and pressures were applied to the Secretary at War, Sidney Herbert, an old friend of Miss Nightingale. She wrote to Herbert to volunteer her services; by coincidence, his letter requesting these services was already on its way to her. Suddenly Florence found herself receiving the support and recognition of her ideas that she had sought for so long. The new development caused her family to rally around and support her. The people of England were openly grateful that a "lady" of Florence's stature was to undertake care of their sons and brothers. She was hailed in the press and in conversations everywhere.

Nightingale was ecstatic but also very realistic. If she succeeded, not only could she relieve the plight of many people less fortunate than she, but she could open up nursing as a socially acceptable occupation for women of her social class. With these goals in mind, she proceeded methodically and cautiously. She chose only a small number of carefully selected women to accompany her. Florence, a politically astute individual, selected Protestant deaconesses as well as Catholic sisters and a few "ladies" who had had little experience caring for the sick. Knowing that she would be able to accomplish very little if she arrived at the war zone unprepared, she arranged to take supplies with her.

After a horrendous trip, the nursing party arrived at Constantinople and proceeded to the barracks hospital. Florence had been careful to be briefed on which doctors might welcome the nurses' assistance and which might oppose it. After the group was settled, Nightingale assigned her nurses at first to work only with the more receptive doctors. After several days, casualties from a major battle began to arrive in such numbers that Florence and her nurses had to help even those doctors who had originally resisted her. Due to their hard work under appalling conditions, the nurses won quick acceptance by most of the doctors and at least the toleration of all. From then on Florence worked systematically on improving conditions in the hospital—securing supplies that were desperately needed, improving diets, seeing to it that soldiers discharged from the hospital had adequate clothing, even hiring local carpenters at her own expense to improve sections of the hospital. The soldiers appreciated the nurses' efforts. Many of them wrote home with lavish praise for Miss Nightingale, telling how she had improved the hospital and how she cared for them often long into the early hours of the morning. Excerpts from the letters found their way into print back home, and she soon was regarded as a heroine. Her own letters home, read to the visitors at her family's estate, only helped to further the Nightingales' social standing. Florence now had become a force with whom to be reckoned. Her popular support among the people of England, her recognition by the Queen, and her family's connections enabled her to get pretty much what she needed or wanted. If there were supplies she could not obtain in any other way, or problems which she could not resolve with the doctors at the front, she simply wrote to her friend, the Secretary at War. She now concentrated her efforts on maintaining the acceptance of the nurses in the hospital.

The greatest crisis of this period came almost accidentally and illustrated the determination and care Florence exercised in pursuing her goals. The Secretary at War, thinking that he was helping, sent a second group of nurses to the hospital without consulting her. The original group had been painstakingly chosen with two basic purposes in mind—to create a group which would be capable of making contributions that could be recognized on their sheer merit, and to ensure that each nurse was an individual with the strength of character to do more than simply follow a doctor's orders. With the new group, Miss Nightingale could not be certain of this. Moreover, the increased size of the nursing corps reduced her ability to control conflicts within it. Florence told her friend that his action had undermined her work and asked that her authority as chief of nurses be reaffirmed. While awaiting a reply, she took great pains to prevent conflict between the original group and the newer nurses, fearing that talk about "women's quarrels" could reduce the nurses' credibility and obstruct her goal of making nursing an acceptable profession for gentlewomen. When her authority was reaffirmed by the government, Florence sent home some of the more dependent problem nurses. She and the others remained until the end of the war, and the experience gave her many ideas for improving health care for England's soldiers. Her accomplishments in all aspects of nursing and health care after her return to England are a matter of history. She carried out all of these projects with the same attention to detail and planning, the same insistence on careful follow-through and documentation. She demonstrated the same willingness to make use of her contacts and influence which had characterized her handling of the Establishment for the Care of Gentlewomen in Sickness and of her assignment in the Crimea.

Nurses, especially female nurses, have benefited immeasurably from Florence Nightingale's persistence and risk-taking. Surely she founded modern nursing, but more than that, she showed us the difference one well-educated, well-connected, wealthy nurse can make if she has the vision and, most of all, the courage to persist. While it is clear that advantages were very helpful to Florence, it would be a mistake to throw up your hands in the belief that change can not be accomplished without them. Let us look at the career of Margaret Sanger.

Sanger as a Leader for Change

If Florence Nightingale was born with a silver spoon, Margaret Higgins Sanger's was barely silver-plated. She was the sixth child of eleven. Although not destitute, the family was not wealthy by any standard. Margaret's father was a stoneworker who carved statues for cemeteries. Her mother, who spent all of her time caring for the family, was forced to manage the household on his limited income plus the earnings of the oldest children. Mr. Higgins despised convention and conformity and believed in the equality of the sexes, even though he may not always have practiced the latter in household matters. He only tolerated organized religion, viewing it as a means by which people maintained discipline. He felt that discipline should come from within oneself. Politically he turned to socialism because he felt that socialism embodied Christian philosophy in practice.

Margaret's father stressed to her and to the other children not to worry about what would happen after death. The important thing, he would say, is what you do in the here-and-now to make other people's lives more decent, and to "leave the world better because you, my child, have dwelt in it." Unafraid to act on his own beliefs, Mr. Higgins invited controversial speakers into their small New York State community of Corning. One such occasion left a deep impression on Margaret. Her father had secured a speaker and rented the town's only hall. On the night of the event she and her father arrived at the hall and found it locked by the local priest, who owned the building and had decided not to permit the speech. Some members in a crowd of onlookers pelted the would-be speaker, Margaret and her father with tomatoes and cabbage; others wanted the visitor to speak. Ignoring the tomatoes, Mr. Higgins stood up straight and announced that the talk would go on in the clearing next to the Higgins' home. The guest delivered his message, but the incident left the family ostracized in the community. The children were taunted as children of the devil, and Catholics were forbidden to order grave monuments from Higgins, worsening the family's already serious financial straits.

One other incident changed young Margaret's life. After being late for school one day, she was repeatedly criticized and severely embarrassed by her teacher. Margaret stormed out of the classroom vowing never to return. Despite lengthy discussions at home, she stuck to her intentions, and finally, in desperation, her two older sisters found a private school and paid her tuition so that she could graduate.

After completing school, Margaret worked as a teacher—just long enough to be sure that this was not what she wanted to do. She considered medical school, but felt she needed more education to enter that field and saw no way of getting it. She decided to enroll in the nursing program at White Plains Hospital. Not long before graduating, she met a dashing young architect and aspiring painter, William Sanger. They married when she was 19. After three children and a few years of comfortable suburban life, they moved into New York City and quickly became caught up in the stimulating life of its more Bohemian groups. The Sanger living room became a gathering place for liberals, anarchists, socialists and members and leaders of the International Workers of the World—the radical so-called Wobblies. Margaret immensely enjoyed the continuing exposure to radical views. Soon she was involved in labor strikes, but always had the idea that something more was needed to truly ease the problems of the poor.

During this period Margaret was working as a nurse. Because they fit best with her family's schedule, she mainly took maternity cases. Increasingly she found herself on Manhattan's crowded and poverty-stricken Lower East Side. Here pregnancy was a chronic condition among the women, and here she first realized the enormous strain this fact placed on their physical, social and economic well-being. Here the desperation of the women was brought home in the suggestions passed mouth-to-mouth for helping "women in trouble"—turpentine, rolling downstairs, inserting slippery elm, shoe hooks, knitting needles. Here she repeatedly heard the same stories of babies born dead, a great relief; of older infants dying, sorrow mixed with relief; of women dying as a result of clumsy abortions. The waste of life seemed senseless, and the destitution seemed inseparably related to the excessive childbearing. Here Margaret gained a social perspective that was to drive her enormous energies for decades to come. The Wobblies were one thing, but what good were desperate labor conflicts over pennies, she asked, if the rapid births of babies gobbled up all the gains and even more?

A single dramatic incident finally crystallized her thinking. Margaret was caring for a 28-year-old woman who had borne three children and who had self-induced her second abortion to keep from having a fourth child. Margaret could only stand by helplessly as the woman died of septicemia. In frustration she vowed to do something about the appalling conditions around her. She decided that the nursing care she was giving merely helped to keep people alive, without dealing with their real problems. Finished with palliatives and superficial cures, she put aside her nurse's uniform to enter the larger social arena and fight for changes. Margaret thought of this as leaving nursing, but today we would simply regard it as moving into another phase of the contemporary nursing role.

Margaret embarked on her new activities with no particular plan. For the moment, she did not even have a clear focus on birth control, except as one important part of a more general impulse to fight against the oppression of the poor and especially of poor women. Because of her experiences on the Lower East Side, she devoted much of her effort to the study of contraception. For several years Margaret studied methods of birth control in the United States. Later she moved to Paris with her husband and the children, she to pursue her study of contraceptive methods in Europe and he to pursue his interest in painting. Some biographers believe that this was a last effort to save a marriage that Margaret had for several years found too confining; if so, the effort failed. Margaret returned to the United States with the children, determined to continue her work.

Back in the United States, Margaret's first big project was to publish a magazine aimed at freeing women from what Margaret had begun to refer to as their biological slavery. She called the magazine the *Woman Rebel* and gave it the slogan, "No Gods, no masters." Women's duty, she declared, was "to look the world in the face with a go to hell look in the eyes, to have an idea, to speak and act in defiance of convention."[1]

Margaret sought help from feminists in starting the magazine, but was refused. Their coolness to the project underscored some differences they had with Margaret. While she focused on the biological liberation best dramatized around the issue of birth control, feminists of the day had other concerns which seemed less important to her. Who cares, she asked, if a woman wears a ring or uses her husband's name instead of hers? She also doubted that a laundress, scrubwoman, cloakmaker or domestic servant worried much about the right to work—for many of the women she knew, a right to leisure might have been more relevant.

Not long after publication of the *Woman Rebel,* the U.S. Post Office notified Margaret that certain issues were unmailable under Section 489 of the Postal Laws and Regulations. For violating the law she could be sentenced to five years in prison and a $5,000 fine. Margaret defiantly mailed the issues and was indicted on nine counts of violation of the statute.[2]

This created a dilemma for her. The magazine and even the indictments had drawn public attention, as Margaret had hoped, to the biological issues. However, the indictments actually dealt with writings on the subject of assassination which had appeared in an article in the magazine. A trial at that time under Section 489 would have diverted attention to issues of radical politics and would not have helped Margaret's cause. She needed to prevent that from happening and to take steps to ensure that the limelight would remain on the birth control issues.

The night before the scheduled opening of her trial she made arrangements for the children and fled, first to Canada and then to

England, under an assumed name. She left behind a letter to the prosecuting attorney and the judge, informing them of her move and stating that she would let them know when she returned to the United States with a better-prepared case.

This action gave Margaret instant publicity as a challenger of the law without calling attention to the real content of the indictments against her. At the same time, Margaret took steps to ensure that the next brush with the law would be the one she really wanted—a conflict with the Comstock Law of 1873, which prohibited the mailing or importation of obscene, lewd or lascivious articles. Her weapon was a pamphlet she had written, *Family Limitation*, giving explicit contraceptive information. As she left, she directed that it be distributed, and more than 100,000 copies were made available.

Her period of exile became a turning point for Margaret. While pursuing her studies of contraception, she was drawn into the influential circles of the Drysdales, guiding spirits of the Neo-Malthusian League. This probirth control group was named for Parson Thomas Robert Malthus, whose dour predictions that population would continuously outpace food supplies had earned him the reputation of being the father of population limitation and family limitation.

The Drysdales introduced Margaret to many of their prominent friends and acquaintances. One of these was Havelock Ellis, the world-renowned sexual psychologist. He became not only Margaret's lover, but also her mentor and coach who spent long hours helping her to analyze her goals and her methods of pursuing them. It was Ellis who persuaded her to narrow her focus and concentrate her energies on her one most burning cause, birth control. Under his guidance, and with the help of the Drysdales' circle of friends, arrangements began to be made for her to speak to more groups of middle-class or prominent women, explaining to them her purposes in publishing the *Woman Rebel*. Margaret now began to appreciate the value of having influential women in her corner. She also pushed forward with her own studies, spending a period in the Netherlands to examine the Dutch approach to birth control. During these months she visited clinics and studied their services, results and data-gathering methods.

Margaret was back in England when she received word that her husband had been jailed for giving a copy of the pamphlet *Family Limitation* to an agent of the New York Society for the Suppression of Vice. The man presented himself as someone who desperately needed the information. Sanger's 30-day sentence received widespread publicity and aroused considerable public outrage. This gave Margaret an opportunity to return to the United States under circumstances which would highlight her real cause. She sailed almost immediately, informing the judge and prosecutor of her return. The drama and public sympathy surrounding her return were heightened several days later when her only daughter, Peggy, became ill with pneumonia and died. Expressions of sympathy and contributions for her legal defense poured in from men and women of all classes across the country. She was asked to take the lead in trying to get the Comstock Law changed.

By now it began to seem possible that Margaret could escape prosecution on the old federal charges. Prominent friends from England wrote President Wilson on her behalf, and some of the letters found their way into the press. Letters and telegrams showered on the judge. Feminists now came to her aid, scheduling speaking engagements for her and packing the audiences with prominent people. Finally, after one postponement of the trial, the charges were dropped.

This experience brought home to Margaret the lessons she had learned from Havelock Ellis and her friends in England. She had begun with the hope, drawn from her early involvement in radical politics and trade unionism, that women of the lower classes would rise up to free themselves of their biological servitude. Now she recognized that she needed a broader support base than radicals and that the poor were generally too exhausted and caught up in their day-to-day struggle for survival to bring about significant change. Rather, real changes required the help of powerful and influential people. She now saw that women of leisure had to be persuaded to listen, women of wealth to give, and women of influence to protest. Margaret's subsequent career was to show that a leader who began without connections to wealth and power could draw those forces to her cause by dramatizing its importance to them.

For the moment, she pursued this objective by means of a national speaking tour. The drama surrounding the court cases had brought her more speaking invitations than she could possibly handle. She took the ones that helped her to reach influential audiences and to stimulate the formation of state birth control associations. In many towns, however, the doors of the halls were closed when she came to speak, reminding Margaret of her childhood experience. These incidents helped increase press attention to her issue and to keep the topic in the public's mind.

Back in New York, Margaret undertook a direct challenge to New

York law by opening a clinic in a low-income section of the city. Besides the publicity such a move guaranteed, her objective was to get a favorable court interpretation of conflicting provisions of state law. One law flatly prohibited anyone from giving out contraceptive information for any reason. Another law allowed physicians to prescribe contraception for the cure or prevention of disease, this latter provision intending to protect men from venereal disease. Margaret wished it used to protect women from ill health resulting from excessive childbearing, and to have the courts recognize women's right to control their own destinies. With her sister Ethel, also a nurse, Margaret opened the clinic in New York's Brownsville section. Here, in separate rooms, they counseled and educated, describing methods of birth control, how to use them and where to buy them. They charged a fee of ten cents for each visit.

The Brownsville clinic operated only briefly before being closed down by a policewoman who posed as a patient. Margaret and Ethel were arrested, convicted and sentenced to 30 days in the workhouse. Ethel was sentenced first. Using an old suffragette technique, she went on a hunger strike. Although the country was at war, the daily reports of her deteriorating condition in jail were front-page news. Even after the warden ordered her to be tube fed, her condition worsened. Finally, prominent people who now supported the cause persuaded the governor to pardon her. Margaret's own jail term passed uneventfully and gave her time to plan her further strategy. Her work would proceed on three fronts—continued public education, the building of an organization to further the cause, and changes in the laws which prevented people from having access to birth control information and services. An appeal of Margaret's own case gave her a partial victory on the legal front. An appellate court judge, while upholding her conviction, broadened the judicial interpretation of "disease" in the state law to include any alteration in the state of the body which caused or threatened pain or sickness. This ruling expanded the use of contraception to cover much more than venereal disease. It still fell far short, however, of Margaret's ultimate goal of allowing women to seek birth control services for social or economic reasons. The ruling did not, as Margaret had hoped it would, result in women getting more information on contraception from their doctors.

On the organizational front, Margaret and her associates were pulling together a new American Birth Control League, with Margaret as its first president. The League had a dramatic beginning as sponsor of the first National Birth Control Conference, scheduled to coincide with a meeting of physicians in New York. When a large crowd of prominent citizens arrived at New York's Town Hall for the final session of the conference, "Birth Control—Is It Moral?" they found the doors locked. A district police official had barred the meeting at the direction of the Archbishop. Needless to say, the incident provided the new organization weeks of free publicity amid charges, countercharges and investigations.

National interest in birth control was now well established, thanks in a large part to Margaret's flair for drama and publicity. To strengthen its acceptance in the scientific community, she turned some of her efforts to the accumulation of scientific data on methods and results. Part of this effort was a clinic, called simply Clinical Research and directed by a female physician. When the first director proved to have relatively low standing with her professional colleagues, Margaret replaced her with Dr. Hannah Stone, a physician of considerable experience who had the respect of other doctors. Margaret also employed a male gynecologist, Dr. James Cooper, a former medical missionary, to speak to medical groups across the country about birth control.

About this time Margaret remarried. Her second husband was J. Noah Slee, who had made a fortune in the 3-in-1 Oil Company, and who promised her that they could do more together than she could do alone. Slee gave time, money and his considerable skills to the cause. His skills were not limited to management. At a time when the importation of contraceptive devices was illegal, he became a big-time bootlegger of diaphragms concealed in oil drums.

Margaret had become a many-faceted institution. She pursued her educational activities, extending them to the international scene with visits to overpopulated nations and the arrangement of international conferences. She pursued her organizational work, sometimes becoming embroiled in infighting about the directions of the organizations. When things went wrong, Margaret's response usually was to withdraw and form a new organization. She always found the constraints of group process too confining for her style and pace, but she recognized it as a necessary nuisance in creating support for the cause.

She pursued her legislative activities, not always successfully. She worked unsuccessfully with one of her groups in Washington for many years seeking changes in the Comstock Law. Though that effort failed, a case pushed by Margaret resulted in a landmark judicial decision which accomplished what Margaret basically had fought for during her entire career. The decision allowed doctors not only to send contraceptives through the mails, but also to prescribe them for patients' general well-being. This was followed quickly by the American Medical Association's announcement to its members that they had a legal right to prescribe contraceptives, and its recommendation that standards be investigated and that contraceptive techniques be routinely taught in medical school.

Margaret felt that she had attained her major goals and from that point on remained in the background. Her achievements, like Florence Nightingale's, were remarkable. She established the American Birth Control League, founded the *Birth Control Review,* opened the nation's first birth control clinic, kept birth control in the public eye in the United States and abroad so that it could be discussed seriously as an issue, sponsored and organized numerous national and international conferences. She is credited with stimulating American medical schools to incorporate birth control into their curricula, and she received numerous awards both at home and abroad. And this is only a partial list.

If her achievements were as awesome as Florence's, Margaret's style was certainly different. Florence had a ready-made power base, and Margaret had to create her own. Florence relied heavily on intellect, reasoned assessment and planning in her approach, while Margaret used an approach which fired people's emotions. Margaret herself often functioned at an emotional level; even then, she instinctively tended to seize the opportunities that arose to dramatize her case and build support for it.

Barton, Breckenridge and Wald as Leaders for Change

History has seen many other nurses who have brought about changes in health care or in their own profession. It was a Civil War nurse, Clara Barton, whose service with the Red Cross in the Franco-Prussian War taught her the value of a nongovernmental organization for disaster and emergency relief. Through her leadership an American Red Cross society was formed and the federal government was persuaded to give it official standing by ratifying the Geneva Convention.

Another nurse, Mary Breckenridge, saw the special needs of people in socially isolated and economically depressed areas. She responded by forming Frontier Nursing Service. In so doing, she also created the nation's first midwifery service and pioneered the then-novel idea that people of the community—the consumers—ought to be included in the planning of their own health care services.

Lillian Wald, a nurse who abandoned plans to become a physician after deciding that she could serve the poor at least as effectively as a nurse, showed one of history's most unique talents for finding opportunities for change in the most unexpected places. Miss Wald was already enrolled in the Woman's Medical College, teaching classes in home nursing for immigrants in her spare time, when she was struck by the critical needs of poorer people for help in matters of health. She ended her medical education and concentrated her energies on developing the "house" on Henry Street which became New York's Henry Street Visiting Nurse Service.

Miss Wald recognized that nursing leadership could penetrate into almost any area related to the health needs of people. In 1909 she became a member of the New York State Immigration Commission and, after an inspection trip to two engineering projects, exposed scandalous exploitation of immigrant workers and their deplorable living and working conditions. Her efforts on these workers' behalf resulted in a crackdown on violations of the labor laws and brought improved health and sanitary facilities to them. Miss Wald did not rest there, but pushed also for a strengthened labor code which was enacted in 1910.

That same year she was appointed to the New York Joint Board of Sanitary Control. On her first inspection tour she found two thirds of the shops she visited lacking adequate fire protection or proper sanitation. Her work on the Factory Visiting Committee resulted in the establishment of mandatory fire drills.

The honors bestowed upon Miss Wald illustrate the breadth of her activities. Smith College in 1930 honored her as the founder of the Henry Street Settlement, organizer of district nursing, originator of the work of the school nurse and of the U.S. Children's Bureau. The Congressional Record in 1934 declared that "her vision and courage have been largely responsible for the legislation resulting in minimum wage, workmen's compensation, the protection of women and children in factories and the abolition of child labor." In 1971 Lillian Wald joined other outstanding Americans in the Hall of Fame for Great Americans.[3]

Kinlein as a Leader for Change

Not all of nursing's change agents, of course, are figures of history. Lucille Kinlein is distinctly contemporary.

The sixth of seven children born to strict German Catholic parents, Miss Kinlein graduated from Notre Dame University with a Bachelor of Arts degree. Turning to nursing partly out of a desire to make a contribution to the American effort in World War II, she entered Catholic University to secure her Bachelor of Science in Nursing degree. She later received her Master of Arts from Catholic University and taught at the Johns Hopkins School of Nursing, Catholic University and Georgetown University.

From the beginning, Miss Kinlein approached nursing as a profession but found herself frustrated by the illogic and inconsistencies she observed in practice. Within a hospital, the nursing care would differ from shift to shift; it would differ from inpatient to outpatient settings, and it would differ when delivered in a doctor's office or in a public health nursing situation. Miss Kinlein kept asking herself: "Why shouldn't nursing care always be the same readily identifiable service?" She concluded that the form of nursing revolved around medical care, and that it differed according to how the physician delivered his service in each health care setting. She felt strongly that this limited her use of her own professional knowledge and skills. Still groping to identify just what nursing was, she was attracted to Dorothea Orem's self-care concept.[4] The pieces fell into place. She now had a concept of nursing that she could use. But the available setting still seemed too confining. She decided to open an office of her own and deliver nursing care from there.

Lucille Kinlein hung out her shingle in May 1971, remaining on the Georgetown faculty because she knew her new endeavor would not support her financially at first. Although elated with her new freedom to practice nursing as she felt it should be practiced, she still had fears. She steeled herself for almost any possible emergency, making certain that she was surrounded by books, including "Emergency War Measures," which she thought should prepare her for almost anything. Soon the clients began to arrive and by October Miss Kinlein had 19 clients.

The resistance she had expected from the medical profession was quick to materialize. At one point, leaders of the Prince George's County Medical Society stated angrily that they were going to redefine nursing to make certain that its practice was under the control of medicine once and for all. Nothing much came of this, however, and overall resistance was not as great as she had expected, mostly taking the form of a wall of silence. There also was another wall of silence which Miss Kinlein had not expected—the silence of other nurses. While the dean and faculty at Georgetown supported the venture from the beginning, Miss Kinlein reports getting a distinct impression that other colleagues in nursing were waiting for her to fail.[5]

That has not happened. After seven years, she has a large practice. She is working with university faculties to develop curricula based on Orem's theory, and is setting up faculty-run satellite clinics to deliver nursing care. Her historic move has encouraged other nurses to enter independent practice and has been another impetus leading the profession to focus more closely on the development of a distinctive nursing theory, on nursing research and on individual state nursing practice acts. The new reality of independent practice also has demonstrated the need to include basic economics and expanded assessment skills in their professional preparation and also has demonstrated the necessity for direct reimbursement for nursing services. At its 1977 national convention, the National League for Nursing presented Miss Kinlein with the Linda Richards Award which recognizes unique pioneering contributions to the profession.

GROUPS EFFECTING CHANGE

While we can identify individual nurses, such as Nightingale, Sanger, and Kinlein, who brought about change with little or no organized support, most nurses have approached needs for major change through group action. Nurses have organized in groups both to obtain the greater support provided by them and to create forums for airing issues and ideas. The choice of group action implies a deliberate tradeoff—individual members give up some of their personal freedom in exchange for the greater strength the group can provide. Often it means that the individual or smaller group must first change the larger group so that its strength can be brought to bear on the smaller group's goals.

American nurses very early recognized the need to work together to further the interests of the nursing profession, its individual members, and consumers of nursing services. This recognition led to the development of formal organizations, such as the American Nurses' Association and the National League for Nursing, and ad hoc groups, such as the National Commission for the Study of Nursing and Nursing Education.

Through more than three quarters of a century of changing social conditions, changing leaders, numerous studies and organizational crises, nursing has wrestled with a group of interrelated, stubborn issues—standards of nursing education, scope and standards of nursing practice, professional autonomy, quality assurance and economic security. Although the terminology and emphases have changed over the years, these issues were and remain the same ones fought for by Florence Nightingale in her struggle to establish nursing as a profession.

Through organized action, nurses have made significant strides in each of these issues. This is true even though the issues have been ones embedded in the basic structure of health care, involving the interests and prerogatives of other, often more powerful, groups. Such issues always have to be faced piece by piece and most often have to be fought over and over again—even sometimes after victory has seemed in hand.

In the case of our earliest nursing organizations, the odds against any progress at all were enormous. Nurses had a fundamentally weak position; they were women in a late Victorian, presuffrage era, and they were subservient, almost menial, helpers in a health care system dominated by male doctors and administrators. This situation left them no choice but to organize, but it also guaranteed that their organizations would start out on a weak footing. As now, a minority of nurses belonged to the earliest nursing organizations. This fact, and the desire to avoid provoking disunity among nurses, forced the groups to adopt conciliatory strategies that were ill-suited to the battle for nursing educational standards and economic security.

Other health care groups, especially physicians, formed their own organizations and refused to join or cooperate with the nursing organizations. Both physicians and hospital administrators opposed nurses' efforts to organize, and adopted active strategies to impede or weaken the nursing organizations and to defeat their goals for reform. Throughout the history of organized nursing, such active resistance by outside power groups has been reinforced by failure of the major nursing organizations to present a united front on many critical issues. In spite of such obstacles, the organized action of nurses has brought progress on the basic issues, but the progress has had a course of ups and downs over the decades.

Through organized action, nurses have demanded and won an increasing voice in the major social, political and economic decisions affecting health care. They have taken an active role in helping to shape national legislation governing labor relations, social security, Medicare, national health planning, federal funding of health care and such pending issues as national health insurance.

The goals pursued by nursing groups in all areas are ones which would be difficult, if not impossible, for nurses to address individually. Achievement of these goals is possible only because of the energy, resources and mutual support inherent in group action.

Change in Nursing Education

Need for Educational Standards Some of the earliest ventures by American nurses into group action were focused on a perceived need for standards of nursing education. Both the need for standards and the need for group action to establish them became clear in the last decade of the 19th century. To appreciate the conditions existing at that time, it might be useful to imagine ourselves transported by time capsule to the year 1890.

We have just selected nursing as our chosen field of work. We learn immediately that nursing is controlled and dominated by hospital administrators and physicians.[6] Although there are no scholarships or other financial aids available to pay for our nursing education, we are assured that we will be allowed to work while we are "trained" to defray the cost of training. If we are very lucky, we might by accident select one of the country's three "Nightingale Schools" of nursing (Bellevue Training School for Nurses, New York; Connecticut Training School, New Haven; or Boston Training School for Nurses at the Massachusetts General Hospital).[7] At one of these schools our "training" would be based on Nightingale's standards, and during the course of our program we would develop an understanding of the art and science upon which nursing practice is based.

Most likely, however, we have not heard of the Nightingale schools and have no reason to think they are any better or worse than the 32 non-Nightingale schools scattered around the country. We choose one of these. Since it has no established entrance requirements, we find ourselves in a heterogeneous group. Some of our schoolmates have high school diplomas; some of them can barely read. We find also that, contrary to Florence Nightingale's hopes, nursing is not highly valued as a career; thus most of our schoolmates come from poor families and have less, rather than more, education.

Our program is unique because each of the 32 programs is unique. There is no uniformity in the length or type of training available. Our program happens to last for two years, but it could be six weeks or three years or anything between. We quickly learn that our education is not as important as hospital needs. If we have a suspicious nature, we might even conclude that the hospital administrator has us pegged as a cheap means to a profitable end for the hospital's owners.

Our apprenticeship in the hospital requires us to work between 12 and 16 hours daily. It's hard work, too, and it leaves us with little time and less energy to study. Most of our "curriculum" is built around the areas where the hospital most needs our labor. The rest of it centers on our instructor's special interests and, perhaps, whims. We can't even find out exactly what qualifications our instructor has. We can be sure, though, that her priorities are clear and that we don't head the list. As one early leader in the development of nursing schools wrote: "The superintendent of a training school is under a threefold obligation: first to the hospital where she works; secondly to the patients who are entrusted to her care; and thirdly to the women for whose education as nurses she is responsible."[8] Our "education" emphasizes such psychomotor skills as scrubbing the floors, washing the linens, fetching things for the doctor and, if time permits, technical skills needed to meet the physical needs of ill patients. This is the substance of our nursing education in 1890.

Coming back to the perspective of nearly 90 years' hindsight, it is easy to see what perceptive nurses already grasped in 1890—nursing "education" presented a pretty grim picture. Enlightened nurses could see the impact of this chaotic situation on the "profession" and on the consumer. They recognized the disparities between Nightingale and non-Nightingale programs in both their educational processes and products. They saw the need for immediate change, and they realized that the necessary educational standards could be established only if nurses worked collectively for them.

This realization was one of the major reasons for the founding of the two major nursing organizations—the American Society of Superintendents of Training Schools for Nurses in 1893 (now the National League for Nursing [NLN]), and the Nurses Associated Alumnae of the United States and Canada in 1897 (now the American Nurses' Association [ANA]). Among the early leaders in organized nursing were Isabel Hampton Robb, the first president of what was to become the ANA; Adelaide Nutting, the first nurse to become a college professor; and Lavinia Dock, a leader in the suffrage movement.[9]

Even before the turn of the century, Robb and other nursing leaders were articulating the need for educational standards in nursing and proposing concrete solutions—a uniform three-year educational base for nursing, increased emphasis on education to attract intelligent women to the profession, direct public support of nursing education and its location in institutions of higher learning rather than in hospitals. The organizations continually reminded nurses and others of the problem. For example, during the presidency of Annie Goodrich (1915–18), the ANA called for a reduction in students' working hours to give them more chance to actually study.

Although the organizations could articulate the concern, they were not able to create immediate progress. This was partly because they were absorbed in their own birth pangs: problems of membership, objectives and procedures of the type that confront all new organizations. It was also partly because problems of nursing education, then as now, did not lie wholly within the control of nurses. Their solution required outside cooperation. Because of critical situations in nursing education and the organizations' inability to move much beyond calling attention to the problems, informal or ad hoc groups were formed to deal with the issues of educational uniformity and standards.

These groups were made up of many disciplines, including nursing. They typically studied nursing education broadly in terms of both its quantity and quality. Foundations often provided the money for such studies, sometimes as a result of appeals by nursing organizations and sometimes as a result of public pressures or the demands of other groups.

Prior to 1920 there were already public expressions of concern about nursing. One concern was a perceived shortage of qualified nurses. This view arose partly because hospitals were staffed almost entirely by students, and patients did not see the graduates—most of whom worked in private duty. There also was demand for qualified public health nurses to meet preventive health care needs. Most nursing school curricula at this time did not even address the nurse's role in prevention.

These concerns, voiced by the public and by physicians, prompted the Rockefeller Foundation in 1918 to underwrite a study of public health nursing and public health nursing education. The study later was broadened to encompass all of nursing education, and resulted in the 1923 publication of what came to be known as the Goldmark report.[10] The report reaffirmed the views of earlier nursing leaders about the shortcomings of nursing education and picked up on many of the earlier recommendations of Robb and others.

Organized nursing responded to the report and implemented some of its recommendations. High school graduation became a general requirement for admission to nursing schools. The students' work week was limited to 48 hours (44 or 40 in some schools). Graduates began to be used more extensively to meet hospitals' staffing needs. Some substandard schools closed. Two collegiate schools of nursing were founded soon afterwards, at Yale (endowed by the Rockefeller Foundation itself) and at Western Reserve (endowed by Frances Payne Bolton). Not only did this follow the Goldmark recommendation that nursing education should move into institutions of higher learning, but it realized a further recommendation that nursing schools seek endowments to assure autonomy from hospital administrations and some base of stable financial support.

Another recommendation, that public health workers should be graduates of a basic course in nursing with added theoretical and clinical work, was picked up eventually in organized nursing's position that the minimum preparation for public health nurses be a baccalaureate degree.

As a further attempt to improve nursing education, the Goldmark report was followed up by an eight-year study of nursing education by the Committee on Grading of Nursing Schools. This group included nurses, physicians, hospital administrators and educators.[11] It planned to publish a classification of nursing schools according to program and product quality; such a publication would have had the effect of forcing the weakest schools to close. In the end the gradings were not published. Many of the target nursing schools closed anyway, even before the committee completed its work, partly because of the ANA's efforts to improve educational standards but mostly because of the economic impact of the Great Depression. When the grading committee's general report finally appeared, it echoed some of the Goldmark report's findings but was considered a disappointment by nurses and had no discernible impact on education.

These first two ad hoc group efforts to improve standards of nursing education raise a number of questions about groups in the process of change. Both committees used extensive research to arrive at their findings, but the impacts were very different. Why was the Goldmark study so much more effective in stimulating change immediately, and in fact even now, more than 50 years later? How did this group inspire such immediate support from nursing organizations? And why did the grading committee's work have such relatively little impact? Why did it shrink from the controversial task it had originally undertaken, the public "grading" of individual schools? Was it related to the character and vested interests of the committee's members, especially the nursing representatives? Was it related to personal commitment to follow up the committee's recommendations? Two nurses on the Goldmark study later became the first deans of the Yale and Western Reserve collegiate schools. Did members of the grading committee have vested interests threatened by their specific findings? Did the differences result from the nature of the tasks—were the criteria for grading nursing schools just too uncertain to justify their publication? Or were the differences the result of timing?

The Goldmark report came at a time when public interest in the subject was high and nursing organizations had cleared the deck for action. The grading committee report, besides lacking the effect it would have had if it had published individual gradings, came at a time when the country was deeply involved in economic woes and everyone, including nursing organizations, had more pressing concerns.

One of the frustrations of reporting historical efforts at change is a lack of documentation of the process. During the 1920s and 1930s—and even today—people did not think consciously about the process of change as such, or at least chose not to record it. The published historical record available to most nurses while strong on reaction to change efforts is weak on the detail of which approaches have worked or failed for change groups, which groups resisted and why the change group and the resisters succeeded or failed in their efforts. Hopefully, as we become more conscious of change as a deliberate, planned process, we will record and publish both successful and unsuccessful efforts so that the process can be carefully analyzed for the benefit of our colleagues. More documentation of the process which initiated the first reports on nursing education and how these reports were then used or blocked might well have helped the series of later studies to be more effective in stimulating change.

Accreditation of Educational Programs While ad hoc groups studied the problem of setting standards for nursing education, others in nursing were developing mechanisms to ensure that standards would be met. As early as 1920 the National Organization for Public Health Nursing began accrediting advanced programs in public health nursing. Twelve years later the handful of collegiate nursing schools formed their own association to explore, among other things, standards for collegiate nursing education. While this association also pursued other goals, it functioned as an accrediting agency for its own membership.[12]

A broader accrediting process was undertaken in the late 1930s by the National League of Nursing Education (NLNE), covering both diploma and collegiate schools. The participating schools shared in the development of the evaluation criteria. They also paid for their own accreditation studies. At a time when most nursing schools were under heavy financial strain, this limited the program's overall impact on nursing education. [13]

In 1948, the National Nursing Accrediting Service (NNAS) was formed under the auspices of the NLNE to replace most of the existing accrediting bodies. The NNAS approach was a modification of the principle of peer review—schools were visited by accreditation teams consisting of nurse educators from other schools and other geographical areas. As part of the procedure, the NNAS published a *Manual of Accrediting Educational Programs in Nursing*. [14] The NNAS also published lists of schools considered "worthy of recognition"—a grading system which identified by omission those schools which might not measure up.

For a time, public health nursing education continued to be accredited by its own original accrediting system, a duplication with NNAS. Another problem of the system was that the NNAS evaluation criteria did not differentiate between degree and diploma programs.

With the establishment of the NLN in 1952, accreditation became an official function of this organization. This voluntary system of accreditation with modifications has remained basically the same. In three decades, this voluntary accreditation program has expanded. Presently there are 290 bacclaureate, 352 diploma and 315 associate degree accredited programs. [15]

Moving into Institutions of Higher Learning   While the initiation and ultimate success of the accreditation process was due to the planning and hard work of these nursing groups, they received a push from another major study of nursing education, the Brown report of 1948. This report was initiated by the National Nursing Council which believed that deficiencies in the quality and quantity of nurses could be traced to the nursing educational system. They sought and received Carnegie Foundation support for a study of the question, "How should a basic professional school of nursing be organized, administered, controlled and financed to prepare its graduates to meet community needs?" [16] Esther Lucille Brown, a social anthropologist, visited 50 nursing schools and held three regional conferences to collect data. She published her findings, interpretations and recommendations in a report, *Nursing for the Future.*

The report echoed the major Goldmark report findings of 25 years earlier, especially in its emphasis on placing nursing education within institutions of higher learning. Brown stressed the need for autonomy and accreditation in nursing schools, and for the public to assume greater financial responsibility for nursing education. She identified a need to clarify the use of the term "professional" in nursing. The report touched off a controversy that still persists to some degree between educators who felt the necessity for collegiate education for professional nursing and those who felt that such a move leaves nurses with inadequate clinical preparation and skills. Two other reports issued in 1948, by Ginzburg and by the Committee on Nursing of the American Medical Association, also supported the push for collegiate nursing education.[17]

The Brown report was pioneering because of its process. It was the first major study of nursing education which included elements of a planned approach to change—assessment, planning, implementation and evaluation. Brown not only analyzed the problems, but laid out a program for implementing her recommendations. This program was partially implemented through the work of a joint Committee for the Improvement of Nursing Service established by the ANA and the NLNE following Brown's suggestion.

The Brown report indirectly provided impetus for one of the most debated innovations in nursing education. This was Mildred Montag's 1951 proposal to prepare nursing technicians. This new health care worker was to be prepared in community colleges to "assist in the planning, implementation and evaluation of nursing care."[18] Montag did not envision administrative responsibilities becoming part of the role of the nursing technician. The program at its inception was considered to be terminal and not a first step toward the baccalaureate degree. By the time Montag's studies of the education and work of nursing technicians were published in 1959, the concept had proven successful in increasing the numbers of nurses and in producing practitioners who filled a real need in health care. The number of programs grew rapidly.

The establishment of these programs had the benefit of preparing practitioners in less time than either baccalaureate or diploma programs and it placed the burden of educational costs on the general public rather than on the patient. Community colleges also benefited by dramatically increased enrollments. Montag's original concept of the nurse technician was soon distorted. Practitioners from these programs, who were initially envisioned as assisting the professional nurse, began to assume functions synonymous with those of the professional nurse in order to fill the gaps in health care delivery. As associate degree graduates responded to the roles they were expected to assume but for which they were not prepared, many educators revamped their curricula to parallel that of the professional nurse. Montag's concept was further distorted with the belief of many educators that the associate degree should be a rung in the career ladder rather than an end.

Up to this point, change efforts in nursing education by groups had succeeded in areas of standardization within types of programs and in achieving successful mechanisms for accreditation. However, efforts at moving education into institutions of higher learning had met with less success, despite the recommendations of a series of major reports over a period of decades.

After 70 years of discussion about placing nursing education in institutions of higher learning, the major nursing organization formally, fully endorsed the principle. This came in 1965, with approval by the ANA of its Committee on Education's Position Paper.[19] The ANA had been steadily moving to assume a greater role in the educational field and the position paper was intended to further this goal by establishing "principles of education" for the profession.

Two problems quickly arose and generated resistance and controversy which all but totally overshadowed the document's basic arguments of preparing future nurses in two levels of collegiate programs. Two-year associate degree programs were to produce nurse technicians and four-year baccalaureate programs were to produce professional nurses. The first problem was that the fate of diploma nursing programs—still the large majority of nursing schools—was dealt with only briefly with the proposal that all diploma schools be linked to colleges and converted either to AD or baccalaureate programs. The sketchy treatment of this group aroused massive resistance among diploma nursing educators and graduates of these schools. The second problem lay in characterizing nurses educated at less than baccalaureate level as technicians. Since 78 percent of all practicing nurses were diploma graduates who had always considered themselves professionals, the report was seen as a slap at the status of the large majority of practicing nurses. The dramatic drop in ANA membership during the next few years may have been caused in part by this move.

In 1967, the ANA tried to soften this political blunder by publishing an interpretive pamphlet pointing out that the legal status of diploma graduates and of students enrolled in diploma programs was not changed.[20] The pamphlet also stated that the intent was not to criticize the past but to focus on future needs of the nursing profession. As late as 1973, the ANA was still trying to heal wounds. In a position approved that spring, it set up mechanisms to ensure that diploma graduates' needs were recognized in ANA programs, to promote upward mobility of diploma graduates and to further clarify the use of the terms "technical" and "professional" in nursing. The statement recognized all registered nurses as professionals. This effort to promote unity in the profession was not totally successful even among diploma graduates. Many interpreted it as a step backward, blurring the technical-professional distinction.

In 1975 the first formal outline of the profession's philosophy, goals and approach to the education of both professional and technical nurses appeared with the ANA's approval of comprehensive *Standards for Nursing Education.*[21] Publication of the standards initiated legislative activity by nurses, since their actual implementation depends on changes in the laws that regulate licensure and practice. Some groups within nursing, especially baccalaureate programs, have been pushing for separate licensure of professional and technical nurses, a move resisted by the Council of State Boards on grounds that existing examinations are "presumed to measure safe and effective practice for *all* registered nurses."[22]

Undaunted, many state nurses associations are laying groundwork to force the issue. The New York State Nurses Association has been one of the leaders with its "1985 Proposal" to require the baccalaureate degree for licensure as a professional nurse and the associate degree for licensure as a "registered nurse associate." The state association has worked with groups working in and representing all educational programs. It proposes that all nurses registered and enrolled in schools of nursing prior to the effective date of the 1985 proposal be "grandfathered" as professionals. Despite continued opposition, the New York State Nurses Association is persisting in its efforts. The goal was reaffirmed at its 1977 convention.[23]

The efforts of formal nursing organizations and of broader, ad hoc commissions and committees to promote and establish high standards of nursing education have been tedious, drawn out and sometimes self-defeating. Unlike change efforts in other areas, attempts to change educational requirements at any level or for any position threaten the status, self-esteem and often the livelihood of hundreds of thousands of nurses and large numbers of educators. These are factors that cannot be ignored, wished away or dealt with superficially. Groups and their leaders effecting changes in education have only erratically applied basic principles of planned change to their efforts—perhaps explanation enough of our slow progress. Yet progress has been made. The chaos and crass exploitation of nursing "students" of the 1890s have been wiped away. The movement of nursing education toward colleges and universities has been a clear and, in recent years, a pronounced trend. Nursing has been established within the mainstream of higher education, although it has yet to develop the full potential of this achievement.

Change in Nursing Practice

Out of the Depths: Licensure The preceding section briefly summarized group efforts of our nursing organizations and broader groups to improve our professional educational system and to bring it into institutions of higher learning. Now we proceed to describe the progress of group efforts to develop and promote higher and more uniform standards for nursing practice. These efforts have spanned the same eight decades—from the 1890s to the 1970s—and have encountered the same obstacles. Nevertheless, as in education, the profession's strides in improving its own practice have been notable. A full appreciation of this fact requires us to return to 1890.

Now we have come to the end of our training as nurses. By this time we have realized that we have been exploited. One of the things we have noticed with apprehension is that there are very few graduate nurses on the staff of the hospital where we trained. We, the students, do most of the work. The full truth hits us at graduation. We learn to our dismay that there are no jobs in the hospital for any of us, and that the work we have been doing is about to be taken over by a new group of students. We turn to the job market outside the hospital and learn some very bleak realities. First, there are almost no staff jobs anywhere. A few public health jobs exist, but the competition for these is fierce. Most of the opportunities which do exist are in private duty nursing. Our competitors for these jobs include "nurses" who began training with us, but dropped out. They also include graduates of schools with programs much briefer than ours. The families from whom we seek employment have no way of knowing who is more qualified than whom. To our dismay, we often see them hiring unqualified dropouts while we cool our heels on the whopping nurse unemployment rolls. It is a doubly deplorable situation: we can not get work, and some of the women who have beaten us to the jobs are endangering their patients because of their lack of preparation. This is our introduction to "professional" nursing practice in 1890.

For nurses who understood the professional principles developed by Florence Nightingale 40 years earlier, this state of affairs was intolerable. They began to unite. Formation of the group which later became the ANA was stimulated by a perceived need for licensing laws to protect the public from unqualified nurses. The organization's first leaders—Robb, Nutting and Dock—went to battle aggressively for these laws.

One of the first things they learned was that major organizational work was needed to pursue such a goal effectively. Because the only well-organized groups of nurses were alumnae associations of nursing schools, the new national organization began as a federation of these associations. Only alumnae association members could belong to the national group.[24]

This organizational arrangement had two major weaknesses. The alumnae groups were not tied to state boundaries, yet the battleground for licensure was the state. Also, the growing mobility of the era resulted in large numbers of nurses living too distant to participate in alumnae association affairs. The logical organizational response was to create state nurses associations, whose membership could include nurses who did not belong to nearby alumnae groups. Many alumnae associations perceived this as a threat to their own strength, and it took several years of debate and compromise to establish the state nurses association as the basic operating unit of the national association.[25] This strategy paid off in the political arena, however, since it enabled such things as practice acts to become a reality more quickly.

Although the first nursing practice act was adopted only in 1903 (in North Carolina), 33 of the 38 states with state nurses associations had practice acts by 1912, and all 48 states had such laws by 1923.[26] In each instance, the original law was permissive—while establishing licensure for nurses, it did not prohibit unlicensed persons from engaging in nursing.[27,28]

Nurses quickly recognized this permissiveness as a serious weakness. Efforts to move from permissive to mandatory licensing laws, which forbid unlicensed individuals from practicing for compensation, have been a slow and arduous process.[29,30] Resistance has come from many sources. As recently as 1971, individuals responsible for a federal report on licensure raised the objection that mandatory laws can be used to exclude individuals who might be capable, but who lack the formal education and other required credentials.[31] Nurses already practicing have feared loss of their livelihoods. Most of these objections have been overcome by providing for various alternative methods of measuring knowledge and skills and by including "grandfather clauses" in the mandatory licensing laws. The first mandatory law was passed in New York in 1938, although because of various resistances it was not implemented until 1947.[32]

Since that time much legislation has been enacted to improve the legal position of nursing. However, there are still problems to be worked out. Some states, for example, lack clear definitions of nursing practice in their acts, and mandatory licensing still is not universal.[33] There is also growing pressure from political leaders, as well as from within nursing, for mandatory continuing education.

Expanding Horizons: The Scope of Nursing Practice Throughout the 20th century nurses have continuously moved toward greater and greater professional autonomy, steadily decreasing our involvement in dependent roles and moving into more interdependent and independent roles. As individual practitioners and groups of practitioners have reached out for expanded roles, organized nursing has followed with supportive group efforts to win recognition for those new roles. Sometimes these group efforts have been vital in establishing new roles, as in follow-up to the Lysaught report of the 1970s. At other times, broader socioeconomic developments have made differences. Two examples are the middle years of the Great Depression, when government programs provided opportunities for expanded nursing responsibilities, and the events surrounding World War II which established nursing's acceptance as a profession in the civil service.

In spite of Florence Nightingale's fondest hopes, it is clear that nursing entered the 20th century as a highly dependent occupation, probably because it was an occupation of women. The submissive nature of nursing was in keeping with the dependent role of women in society generally. It was probably no accident that nurses' responsibilities in the hospital placed emphasis on the same areas emphasized in women's responsibilities in the home—scrubbing, cleaning, "fetch-and-carry" for men who wielded authority.

The decrease in dependent roles of nursing and the increase in interdependent and independent roles closely followed improvements in educational standards that nursing groups had accomplished. Additionally, however, role changes occurred as increased responsibilities were forced on nursing by changes in society and in health care. Among the key factors were changes in health care technology which moved physicians out of primary care and into increasingly narrow specialties. The equipment and other products of new technology which transformed the health care environment, especially in hospitals, and required new and more demanding skills of nurses in that environment served as additional factors. Population growth and improved health care standards, which placed greater demands on the entire health care system and at the same time increased the responsibilities of the health professions, played a part. Sheer economics, which has forced health care gradually out of a purely medical, curative model into a preventive, health-maintenance model more consistent with traditional professional values in nursing, is playing a critical role. All of these factors promoted growing autonomy of the nursing role in the community, and a more collaborative role in hospitals and other organized health care settings.

Recognition of changes in nursing roles came in the early-1970s in the work of the interdisciplinary National Commission for the Study of Nursing and Nursing Education. This body, an outgrowth of recommendations by an earlier consultant panel to the U.S. Surgeon General, was cosponsored by the ANA and the NLN. It resulted in a publication known familiarly as the Lysaught report. Of the four central recommendations in the report, two were directly aimed at furthering independent functioning:

1. That government and private agencies provide funds for expanded research on nursing practice and its impact on the "quality, effectiveness and economy of health care."[34]

2. That a National Joint Practice Commission and state counterparts be established by medicine and nursing to explore the "congruent" roles of physician and nurse in health care.

The recommended joint practice commission was established by the ANA and the American Medical Association in 1972, followed by the creation of many state-level counterparts. The basic principle of joint practice, as developed concretely through activities of these bodies, is nurses and physicians collaborating as colleagues to provide patient care. Each brings his own training and skills into a practice in which the planning for patient care is done jointly and each professional assumes responsibility and accountability for his own actions within the jointly developed plan. While the joint commission deals mostly with practice in the community, it has undertaken a major study financed by the W. K. Kellogg Foundation to explore new, collegial relationships of physicians and nurses in hospital settings. Four selected hospitals across the United States have initiated projects which include a program of primary nursing care, an integrated patient-record system, joint nurse-physician evaluation of patient care, and a joint practice committee. This project is to culminate in 1980 with the publication of guidelines for establishing joint practice in hospitals.[35]

The Loeb Center for Nursing and Rehabilitation in New York is another leading example of interdependent nurse-physician collaboration in a tertiary care setting. This unit is nurse administered. The Loeb Center's objective is to demonstrate that high quality nursing care given solely by registered nurses offers a supportive service to people in the postacute phases of their illness. It is the nursing intervention which reportedly enables them to recover sooner and to leave the center with an ability to cope with themselves and what they must face in the future. The center creates a setting in which nurses can develop their abilities and role without being burdened by nonnursing functions. The arrangement has been praised as one which demonstrates the value of nursing and its differences from medicine, but which shows "how nursing and medicine need to and can work interdependently."[36]

Beyond the interdependent roles developing through trials of joint practice, nurses have begun to function independently as family nurse clinicians, pediatric nurse practitioners and nurse midwives to mention but a few. In each expanded role, nurses have worked successfully to expand the quality and availability of primary health care. To help establish quality control and promote the development of these independent roles, the ANA has established a program of certification. This program formally recognizes individuals who have met special criteria for individual achievement and superior performance in their specialties. The ANA is currently sponsoring a broad study on certification, licensure and accreditation in nursing and nursing education. This study ties in with the general issue of quality assurance in nursing.[37]

Assuring the Quality of Nursing Care Nursing, as one author suggests is "at the beginning of an organized, large-scale planned approach to ensuring the quality of its services."[38] "Quality assurance" is simply the general term for those programs by which we seek to measure the excellence of our services; its goal is to assure ourselves, the consumer, and the public that some specified level of quality of care is provided.

To accomplish this, we must evaluate the care received by clients against criteria designed to measure the effects of that care on the clients. Effects are judged in relation to the use of resources, professional time, equipment, supplies and to the environment in which care is given. A quality assurance program asks the questions: Is the nursing care effective? And, is it *cost*-effective?

The nursing literature identifies three major variables as relevant in this measurement:

1. The nature of the setting and/or the conditions under which nursing care is delivered—the *structure,* organization or environment in which it takes place.

2. The specific practices or interventions that constitute professional nursing—the *process* of nursing itself.

3. The effects of 1 and 2 on the consumer—the actual *outcome* of nursing intervention for the client.[39]

There is continued debate and discussion within nursing as to which variables should be studied or viewed as most important for quality assurance. How precisely do structure, process and outcome relate to each other?

Concern for the quality of nursing is not new. A report to the Massachusetts legislature in 1850 stated that "bad nursing often defeats the intention of the best medical advice, and good nursing often supplants the effects of bad advice."[40]

In 1858, Florence Nightingale established standards for nursing practice. Her primary emphasis in quality assurance was the structural criteria that she observed patients needed to recover. "Since we don't know what causes disease, our job is to place the patient in the best condition for nature to act upon him."[41] Miss Nightingale further decried the "mindless application of process." "It is not for the sake of piling up miscellaneous information or curious facts, but for the sake of saving life and increasing health and comfort."[42] She touches on outcomes as something few people can measure except for the final outcome. "There is no more silly or universal question scarcely asked than 'Is he better'?"[43]

Despite Florence's efforts in establishing nursing practice standards, Isabel Hampton Robb, 35 years later, was still to decry the lack of standards in nursing care in the United States. She declared that ". . . 'trained nurse' may mean anything, everything, or next to nothing . . . and public criticism is frequently justly severe upon our shortcomings."[44]

Since early in the century, increasing attention has been directed toward assuring the quality of care for patients within hospitals.

From its founding in 1913 the American College of Surgeons worked to develop means of ensuring excellence in hospital care; from its beginning efforts there eventually grew the Joint Commission on Accreditation of Hospitals, whose basic standards for hospitals were issued in 1970; these standards primarily emphasizing structure were revised in 1973.[45] The Joint Commission also has expanded to explore standards of quality and quality assurance for other settings.

In 1972, the American Hospital Association's Quality Assurance Program spelled out an approach stressing the use of audits, to assure quality care. It also urged the creation of separate committees within each hospital, one for Medical Audit (including other professionals' own peer review audits) and the other for Utilization Review.[46] The same year, amendments to Title XI of the Social Security Act created Professional Standards Review Organizations (PSROs) charged with reviewing Social Security-funded health care with respect to medical necessity, quality of care, and whether care was given at the level most economical for the patient's need. The PSROs are responsible for review of all institutional services and the practices of all professionals delivering these services.[47] In 1972 the Joint Commission published its "Procedure for Retrospective Patient Care Audit in Hospitals" which suggested outcome audit for identifying problems, backed up by process audit to help solve the problems once identified.[48]

All of these efforts have taken impetus from a trend that has been developing for half a century, most markedly since the advent of Medicare and Medicaid, to provide consumers and their representatives with more clout to enforce accountability on providers of service. In health care, a growing concentration of consumer power in insurance carriers, labor unions and government has literally forced greater attention to the quality of service. The effects have been felt first and most strongly in medicine and institutions, but are quickly becoming felt also by the nursing profession.

Throughout their history, nursing organizations have shown concern for ensuring the quality of nursing service. The ANA's concern has taken the form of programs for state licensure; the development of educational standards for preparing individuals to practice; publication of standards for practice and for organized nursing services (the ANA's standards for nursing practice were published in 1973, emphasizing structure and process); a program of certification; support of research in nursing care, and the development of councils of practitioners.[49]

In an address to the Joint Institute of the American Hospital Association (AHA) and the ANA, Virginia Paulson pointed out that programs and tools can be used to develop models of quality assurance.[50] It is the prerogative of the professional association to develop such a model. Just as the ANA has taken the leadership in establishing standards and guidelines for professional review systems and positions on nursing professionals' accountability, local leadership needs to further develop methods for implementing these guidelines.[51]

The NLN also has been consistent in its concern for the quality of care. Since its establishment, this organization has involved consumers continuously in all major decision-making processes. Their program of accreditation through criteria development and peer review documents NLN's concern. Position statements directed toward improving quality care have been ongoing. Tools for cost-effectiveness and quality control were a product of this organized group long before the demand for them. Dr. Virgil Slee, a former nonnurse member of a league committee, helped to develop the *Quest for Quality*, a document used as a prototype for many hospitals as they developed nursing audit procedures.[52] Continuing education workshops by the NLN have often been directed at developing methods and tools for improving quality.

Both the ANA and NLN have helped to define, promote and evaluate tools for assuring excellence in nursing. At the same time they have not overlooked the fact that excellence in nursing depends on the working conditions and economic status of nurses.

Economic Security and Collective Bargaining Economic security and welfare issues have always been a major theme in organized nursing, and the efforts of our organizations to effect change in these areas have typified the seesaw character of basic change.

We have already seen the economic plight of nurses at the turn of the century, when nurses, being primarily women who had few other employment opportunities, were a cheap and readily exploitable source of labor. Their miserable economic status showed itself clearly in the second decade of the century when the ANA, hoping to win shorter work days for student nurses, proposed an eight-hour work day for graduates. At that time most graduates were in private duty, where 12-hour and 16-hour shifts and even 24-hour demand work schedules were usual. These nurses saw shorter hours as a cut in pay.[53] Their vigorous resistance to the ANA proposal pointed up the deep-seated feelings of economic insecurity in the profession.

Another hotly debated topic during this phase of nursing's development was the issue of the nurse registries. Registries—lists of nurses available for employment—were the private duty nurse's key to finding work. Often, however, they were controlled by non-nurses. Some were run by medical societies which placed more emphasis on nurses' compatibility with physicians than on their individual nursing competence. Some were commercial and included names of individuals with little or no training. Many were run by nursing schools. These tended to promote the sponsoring schools' own graduates, excluding other nurses or dropping them to the bottom of the lists.[54]

Years of vigorous efforts by organized nursing produced only very modest results in changing this situation, highlighting the resistance offered when livelihood is threatened. They were able to generate awareness among nurses of the problem, but not to obtain agreement on the ANA's proposed solution—central registries under the control of the profession. That goal was realized only in some local areas where district nurses associations succeeded in establishing professionally controlled registries and winning public acceptance of them. The turmoil surrounding registries died down only when private duty nursing faded as the economic mainstay of nurses.[55] It could resurface in the future as more and more nurses enter independent roles. (Who in your local area currently has a listing of nurses working in expanded roles?)

The skirmishes over working hours and registries were only the beginning of nursing organizations' efforts to cope with profound economic and welfare issues impeding development of the profession. During the Depression, when they were themselves plagued with financial problems, the organizations were able to make some inroads on the tremendously high levels of unemployed nurses by promoting new jobs in hospitals and in the many government-sponsored programs that sprang up. The conditions of this period laid the basis for nursing's most dramatic break with tradition, its sharp move in the mid- to late 1940s into collective bargaining.

Three factors set the stage for the ANA to become the nation's first professional organization to dip its toes into collective bargaining. The first was the rock-bottom economic circumstances of nurses, which had lasted through the war years despite a nursing war effort that had earned the profession tremendous respect and praise, but not increased salaries. In 1946, general duty nurses were earning about $2,000 per year for a work week averaging more than 44 hours under work conditions that made it nearly impossible to

provide truly quality nursing care.[56] The second factor that encouraged collective bargaining was the National Labor Relations
Act of 1935. This act placed most of the nation's employers (including, at that time, hospitals) under the purview of the National
Labor Relations Board and required them to bargain collectively
with employee groups. It also prohibited them from interfering
with efforts of employees to organize themselves.[57] By the late
1930s, labor unions had begun to organize health care workers, and
were making serious overtures to nurses. Attempting to protect the
unity of the profession and still respond to nurses' economic welfare, leaders in a few state nurses associations began to experiment
with collective bargaining. The California State Nurses Association,
especially, enjoyed modest success functioning as a bargaining unit
for groups of its members. Efforts at collective bargaining were
greeted initially with skepticism among many nurses, who
regarded it as "unprofessional" or even "unladylike" or who
equated it with the use of strikes. The ANA felt the use of strikes
was "incompatible with nursing service ideals."[58] However, the
ANA in 1946 overwhelmingly approved an Economic Security Program which included collective bargaining as a cornerstone of efforts to ensure "that nurses have a voice in determining their employment conditions, that nursing salaries are appropriate to
nursing responsibilities, and that employment conditions are of the
kind to enable nurses to give a high quality of care."[59] The resolu-
tion called upon state associations to pursue the twin goals of a 40-
hour week and "adequate" salaries by collective bargaining.
Members who voted for this program were assured that the use of
strikes would not be necessary.[60]

Only a year later, collective bargaining for nurses received a
major setback when the Taft-Hartley Act of 1947 excluded nonprofit
hospitals from the bargaining requirements of the National Labor
Relations Act. The ANA had lobbied vigorously against this provision, but lobbying by the American Hospital Association pre-
vailed.[61] Its enactment left nurse associations without a clear legal
weapon to force hospitals to the bargaining table if they refused to
come voluntarily. The ANA tried to fill the breach by moral sua-
sion. In an idealistically phrased policy adopted in 1950, ANA dele-
gates declared that nurses should not use the strike as a weapon of
collective bargaining but that employers had special obligations to
bargain with them.[62] Most employers obviously saw it differently.
Successful negotiations of contracts continued to be rare. The slow
progress on this front also may have been due in part to continued

division among association members about the use of collective bargaining. Repeated efforts were raised within ANA to drop collective bargaining. There also was resistance, especially by nurse administrators, to efforts by state associations to seek legislation bringing nonprofit hospitals under the purview of state fair labor practices laws.[63] Despite the resistance, state nurses associations in several states were able to get these laws passed.

With or without these laws, the number of state associations which had successfully negotiated contracts through collective bargaining grew from only eight in 1963 to 32 in 1973.[64] Progress was directly related to the adoption of increasingly militant techniques, usually short of actual strike, to force employers to bargain and to win improvements in salaries and working conditions. These techniques included picketing, "sick-outs," and even mass resignations. As in earlier decades, the California Nurses Association was among the leaders.

The use of militant techniques by restless nurses reached a crescendo stage in 1966. That year in California nurses used these techniques to win major concessions for most nurses working in both the San Francisco and Los Angeles areas. In the Bay area, one small hospital met nurses' demands just before the effective date of mass resignations. Another settled three days after the nurses actually left their jobs. These incidents lent support for the mass resignation threats of 1,900 out of 2,000 nurses employed at 31 other Bay area hospitals. The hospitals agreed to fact-finding on major issues to avert the resignations.[65]

Nurses at six city-operated hospitals in San Francisco by city ordinance could not receive pay increases except in emergencies. They created an "emergency" by staging a one-day mass sick call that left only skeleton staffs to handle urgent patient needs. They received their pay increases.[66] Nurses employed at California state hospitals staged mass rallies at the state capitol to win improved salaries and working conditions.[67] In Idaho, a small community hospital was forced to close for 16 days, transferring patients to another hospital, when nurses resigned en masse. The nurses quickly were rehired at their old positions with salary increases.[68] Some of the discontent attracted renewed union efforts to organize nurses. Under this pressure, state nurses associations began to disregard the no-strike pledge. It was renounced in 1966 by California and Pennsylvania.[69]

In 1968 the ANA, confronted with the marked successes of militant techniques in California and elsewhere, and already undercut by state associations' increasing rejection of the no-strike policy, approved the use of strikes as a less drastic technique than mass resignations. The ANA also increased its field staff to provide support to state associations in collective bargaining, and approved a salary goal of $7,500 per year for nurses, two thirds higher than the national average of only two years earlier.[70] Strikes have been used by nurses selectively and successfully since then, under conditions which provide sufficient staffing to protect patients from harm. A final obstacle to fully effective use of collective bargaining techniques was removed in 1974. Congress amended the Taft-Hartley Act to place nonprofit hospitals once more under jurisdiction of the National Labor Relations Board's collective bargaining mandates. Over the intervening 27 years, American Hospital Association resistance had been weakened by two trends pushed in part by organized nursing groups. First they succeeded in changing some state labor laws which included hospitals under terms that varied from state to state and complicated AHA's efforts to work on behalf of its members. Second, nurses and others succeeded in winning the right to bargain locally even though it was not necessarily guaranteed by law.[71]

With collective bargaining well established as a tool for improving nurses' conditions, state nurses associations have turned increasingly to its use for dealing with issues of practice in addition to economics. A recent strike in 15 of 16 Seattle hospitals resulted in a new contract providing not only salary increases over three years, but also several changes to terms of practice. The new contract specifies that all members of the nurse practice committee will be elected by staff nurses. Previously 50 percent were elected by supervisors. This committee meets with management to discuss practice issues. The contract also limits shift rotation to every 14 days by mutual consent of the employee and management and guarantees two of four weekends off.[72]

In Tennessee, nurses employed in the Memphis-Shelby County Hospital Authority also recently won a new contract. This one was especially difficult to negotiate because the city ordinance under which the previous contract was signed in 1974 had been knocked down in court. The 1974 Taft-Hartley Amendments did not apply since the nurses were publicly employed. The nurses asked the Tennessee State Nurses Association to represent them and agreed to stick together as a group. Their initial strike vote failed to bring the hospital authority into bargaining, and so did a subsequent intervention by physicians. Only on the eve of the strike date, when it became clear that the nurses intended to go through with it, did the authority come to the table. As in Seattle, the resulting contract provided both improved pay and improved practice conditions. One especially noteworthy protection of the quality of nursing care was a provision that nurses assigned to special care units must be provided with orientation, and that nurses cannot be assigned to units for which they are not prepared.[73]

A recent issue of the *American Journal of Nursing* carried articles about Rhode Island nurses bargaining for better staffing standards and tighter medication policies in state hospitals, New York nurses voting to abandon a no-strike policy, and Minnesota nurses resisting a county health program reorganization that would affect the professional nature of nursing practice.[74] All of these are representative of the growing use of collective bargaining to determine issues of staffing and quality of care, to establish the right to strike or engage in other forms of work stoppages, and to promote the autonomy of the profession. Nurses have become aware of the power of their own collective action.

In reviewing the change efforts of individuals and groups within nursing since 1890, it is obvious that some have been more successful than others. Individuals chose different arenas in which to effect change and varied in their style and approach. Group attempts at change varied in their success perhaps due to social or economic conditions of the time, lack of planning, timing of the change, character of the smaller group attempting the change, or the overwhelming threat that change had on the affected group. Quite obviously, our attempt has not been to review all the attempts of groups or of individuals to effect change in nursing, but rather to highlight some examples so that we might learn from these attempts as we analyze the process of change.

Florence Nightingale's original goals for nursing were to establish it as an acceptable vocation for women of her class, as a discipline recognized for its own knowledge and contribution, as a vocation that provided economic security for women and as an avenue for improving conditions of the poor. The original goals of organized nursing in the United States at the turn of the century were to protect the public from incompetent practitioners, to improve and standardize educational preparation and to improve economic security. When we look at modern nursing in light of these goals, we have to ask ourselves, "How far have we come?"

We have made significant progress in many areas and as nurses we must have tremendous pride in what individual members and our associations have done in improving health care delivery to the country and improving the profession. At the same time, we must address the areas that remain weak.

Should it have taken 90 years for nursing to have arrived at this point in educational preparation of nurses? The public still seems to be as confused as it was at the turn of the century or at the time of the Surgeon General's report about the educational preparation of nurses. Likewise, should it have taken 90 years for the average salary of nurses to equal that of men working as *helpers* in the skilled trades in factories?[75]

Can we afford to continue wasting our energies by allowing the larger issues in health care planning, delivery and payment to be decided by others or a few overworked nursing leaders while we argue such issues as nursing service vs. nursing education, the names for each level of educational preparation and whether we should call the recipients of our care patients or clients?

Each of us can identify scores of areas where we as individuals and as groups remain frustrated and need to bring about change more quickly. However, the time is long past when we can become frustrated, throw up our hands, raise our voices and blame each other and our nursing organizations for our ineffectiveness. As professionals we cannot escape the responsibility we each bear in changing these situations. Each of us must measure our own functioning. We have much more to do.

References

1. Margaret Sanger, *Margaret Sanger, an Autobiography*. New York: Dover Publications, 1971, p. 107.
2. *Ibid.*, p. 108.
3. Josephine A. Dolan, *Nursing in Society*. Philadelphia: W. B. Saunders Company, 1973, p. 317.
4. Dorothea Orem, *Nursing-Concepts of Practice*. New York: McGraw-Hill Book Company, 1971.
5. Lucille Kinlein, Personal Interview. June 1977.
6. Jo Ann Ashley, *Hospitals, Paternalism and the Role of the Nurse*. New York: Teachers College Press, 1976.
7. Marilyn Rawnsley, "The Goldmark Report: Midpoint in Nursing History." *Nursing Outlook* (June 1973): 38.
8. Jerome Lysaught, *An Abstract for Action*. New York: McGraw-Hill Book Company, 1970, p. 28.
9. Dolan, *Nursing in Society*, p. 284.
10. C. E. A. Winslow and Josephine Goldmark, *Nursing and Nursing Educa-*

tion in the United States. New York: The Macmillan Company, 1923, pp. 10–25.

11. Lyndia Flanagan, *One Strong Voice—The Story of the American Nurses Association.* Missouri: The Lowell Press, 1976, p. 83.

12. Gwendoline MacDonald, *Development of Standards and Accreditation in Collegiate Nursing Education.* New York: Teachers College, Columbia University Press, 1965, pp. 63–65.

13. *Ibid.,* pp. 65–70.

14. *Ibid.,* pp. 68–70.

15. Helen Yura, National League for Nursing. Personal Communication. December 21, 1977.

16. Dolan, *Nursing in Society,* p. 277.

17. *Ibid.,* pp. 278–279.

18. Mildred Montag, *The Education of Nursing Technicians.* New York: G. P. Putnam and Sons, 1951.

19. American Nurses' Association, "Educational Preparation for Nurse Practitioners and Assistants to Nursing: A Position Paper." New York: The Association, 1965.

20. Flanagan, *One Strong Voice,* p. 244.

21. Lucie Young Kelly, *Dimensions of Professional Nursing,* ed. 3. New York: The Macmillan Company, 1975, p. 365.

22. *Ibid.,* p. 165.

23. "NYSNA Votes to Rescind No-Strike Policy." *American Journal of Nursing* 77, 12 (December 1977): 1888.

24. Flanagan, *One Strong Voice,* p. 32.

25. *Ibid.,* p. 47.

26. Teresa E. Christy, "The First 50 Years." *American Journal of Nursing* 71 (September 9, 1971): 1779.

27. Helen Creighton, *Law Every Nurse Should Know,* ed. 3. Philadelphia: W. B. Saunders Company, 1975, pp. 9–10.

28. Kelly, *Professional Nursing,* p. 285.

29. Creighton, *Law Every Nurse Should Know,* p. 10.

30. Kelly, *Professional Nursing,* p. 285.

31. *Ibid.,* p. 285.

32. *Ibid.,* p. 286.

33. Creighton, *Law Every Nurse Should Know,* p. 8.

34. Lysaught, *Abstract for Action,* pp. 156–160.

35. "Kellogg Foundation Grant Funds Joint Practice Project in Hospitals." *American Journal of Nursing* 77, 10 (October 1977): 1543, 1552.

36. Ferres Susan Bowar, "Loeb Center and Its Philosophy of Nursing." *American Journal of Nursing* 75 (May 5, 1975): 810–815.

37. "Study of Credentialing Launched." *American Journal of Nursing,* 76, 12 (December 1976): 1893–1895.

38. Mary F. Woody, "Where is Nursing in Quality Assurance?" *Quality Assurance: Models for Nursing Education.* New York: National League for Nursing, 1976, p. 33.

39. R. K. Dieter Haussmann and Sue T. Hegyvary, "Monitoring the Quality of Nursing Care." *Quality Assessment and Patient Care*. New York: National League for Nursing, 1975, p. 12.
40. Lemuel Shattuck, et al., *Report of the Sanitary Commission of 1850*. Cambridge, Mass.: Harvard University Press, 1948, p. 224.
41. Florence Nightingale, *Notes on Nursing*. Philadelphia: J. B. Lippincott Company, 1946, p. 70.
42. *Ibid.*, p. 73.
43. *Ibid.*, p. 59.
44. Mary M. Roberts, "Nursing of the Sick." *American Nursing: History and Interpretation*. New York: The Macmillian Company, 1954, p. 22.
45. Woody, "Where Is Nursing," p. 35.
46. *Ibid.*, p. 35.
47. Minnie H. Walton, "Quality Assurance in Health Care." *Quality Assurance: Models for Nursing Education*. New York: National League for Nursing, 1976, p. 29.
48. Joint Commission on Accreditation of Hospitals, *Procedure for Retrospective Patient Care Audit in Hospitals*. Chicago: The Commission, 1972.
49. American Nurses Association, *Standards of Nursing Practice*. Kansas City: American Nurses Association, 1973.
50. Walton, "Quality Assurance," p. 31.
51. Woody, "Where is Nursing," p. 31.
52. National League for Nursing, *Quest for Quality: A Self Evaluation Guide to Patient Care*. New York: National League for Nursing, 1966.
53. Christy, "The First 50 Years," p. 1780.
54. Flanagan, *One Strong Voice*, p. 103.
55. Christy, "The First 50 Years," p. 1781.
56. Barbara G. Schutt, "The Recent Past." *American Journal of Nursing* 71 (September 9, 1971): 1786.
57. Thomas P. Herzog, "The National Labor Relations Act and the A.N.A.: A Dilemma of Professionalism." *Journal of Nursing Administration* 76: 34–36.
58. Norma K. Grand, "Nightingalism, Employeeism and Professional Collectivism." *Nursing Forum* 71: 289–299.
59. Kelly, *Professional Nursing*, p. 368.
60. Schutt, "The Recent Past," p. 1786.
61. *Ibid.*, p. 1788.
62. *Ibid.*, p. 1788.
63. Anne Zimmerman, "Taft-Hartley Amended: Implications for Nursing." *American Journal of Nursing* 75: 284–292.
64. Barbara G. Schutt, "Collective Action for Professional Security." *American Journal of Nursing* 73 (September 9, 1973): 1946–1951.
65. "California Nurses Agree to Fact Finding." *American Journal of Nursing* 66 (September 9, 1966): 1901.
66. "Sick Call to Cure Ills." *American Journal of Nursing* 66 (October 1966): 2134.

67. "California Nurses Picket State Capitol." *American Journal of Nursing* 66 (November 1966).

68. "Action on Salaries, Use of Mass Resignations Increasing." *American Journal of Nursing* 66 (June 1966).

69. "Pennsylvania Nurses Rescind No-Strike Pledge." *American Journal of Nursing* 66 (November 1966).

70. Flanagan, *One Strong Voice*, p. 262.

71. *Ibid.*, pp. 262–267.

72. "Seattle Strike Settled with Three Year Contract." *American Journal of Nursing* 76 (November 11, 1976): 1734.

73. Rosemary Bowman, Executive Director of the Tennessee Nurses Association, Personal Interview. June 1977.

74. "Rhode Island State Hospital Nurses Struggle for More Nurses, Tighter Medication Policy." *American Journal of Nursing* 77 (December 1977): 1885, 1904.

75. U.S. Department of Labor, Bureau of Labor Statistics 1977. *Industry Wage Survey: Hospitals, August 1975–January 1976,* and *Area Wage Surveys: Selected Metropolitan Areas 1975.*

TWO

We Have More To Do

We have done much. As leaders for change, we have brought
health care to people in rural areas where care had been nonexis-
tent; we have provided for continuity of care through the visiting
nursing service; we have helped to create emergency services for
people through the Red Cross effort; we have improved the health
and safety of industrial workers, and we have done a great deal to
assure the public of quality and professionalism in its health care.
As providers of a unique and vital service we have made one tremendous contribution to meeting the health care needs of this nation, and we continue to do so.

For more than a century we have provided care to hundreds of
thousands of fighting men in every skirmish and war this country
has seen. We continue to provide care to people in rural areas and
many urban neighborhoods, often as the only health care providers.
We continue to bridge the gap between inpatient, outpatient and
home care, the latter an increasingly important service as people are
discharged earlier from hospitals. As technology has provided medicine with newer, more complicated and more sophisticated
methods of diagnosing and treating illness, we remain the caring
link between the hardware of that technology and the human needs
of the client and his family. We remain the health care providers
who relate not just to the person's lungs, liver, heart and housing,
but to all of him physically and emotionally, and to all of him in the
context of his social environment. And we provide these caring ser-

vices not only in the hospitals, but in schools, industries, nursing homes, home health agencies, neighborhood health centers, the homes and haunts of our clients. Not only do we give service in all these settings, but in most of them we represent the largest group of health care workers.

Think for a moment of the impact on the nation's health care of just two days without nurses.

Because we provide a unique service, because we provide it in so many settings, and because collectively we are closer to health care clients than any other health care providers, we are in a key position to more effectively direct the delivery of health care and to receive a greater share of the recognition and rewards in giving that care.

PROBLEMS IN THE HEALTH CARE SYSTEM

The American people are becoming more and more disillusioned with their health care system. Its costs are incredibly high and rising. Health care is big business in the United States, costing more than national defense. In 1975, Americans spent an average of $547 per person for health care and related products and services.[1] But that simple statistic scarcely hints at the degree to which health care is a major financial burden for many families. A catastrophic illness can reduce a middle-income family to poverty in less than two years. A study by Cancer Care, Inc. and the National Cancer Foundation showed that caring for a patient with advanced cancer costs the family approximately $22,000. Of the families in the study, only 40 percent received health insurance payments of more than $10,000 to help cover these staggering costs.[2]

Health insurance, while aimed at helping individuals and families cope with their individual high costs of illness, has actually increased overall health care costs. A typical American's overall health insurance coverage encourages him to use higher cost services where lower cost services would do. It excludes virtually all preventive services, excludes many outpatient services, excludes mental health coverages that could reduce the incidence, severity and ultimate costs of treating psychosomatic illnesses, excludes nursing services except under the umbrella of overall hospital charges, and often forces patients to enter hospitals to be covered for physicians' services that could be performed elsewhere. People often prefer to be admitted to hospitals even when it is not medically necessary because their insurance pays only for services in hospitals. Hospital insurance also has encouraged inefficiency; it simply has not provided significant incentives for controlling costs.[3]

Hospital costs clearly are the major factor in our soaring health costs. Some of these can be traced to an excessive increase in the number of hospital beds in many areas and to needless duplication of costly equipment, specialized facilities and services—sometimes purely to enhance the prestige of individual hospitals or their boards. Too many beds means inefficient occupancy rates. If overhead costs are divided among 50 patients instead of 80, it stands to reason that daily rates have to go up. Similarly, too many open heart surgery units means that some will be underused. This not only drives up the total overhead of hospital care, but also reduces average quality of care, since units used only occasionally cannot deliver the same quality of service as those whose capabilities are sharpened by daily use. In medicine, unlike most fields, new technologies often increase manpower needs instead of decreasing them. This has been another force pushing costs upward. And growing unionization also has been increasing the average cost of this increasing manpower. All of these factors have made the cost of health care a frightening factor in the everyday lives of many Americans.

For many Americans, access to health care is as great a problem as its costs. In urban areas there are poor populations who have almost no access to care. One section of New York City, for example, had 50 doctors serving a population of 25,000 just 25 years ago. Today there are four doctors for 50,000 people.[4] More affluent people may have the money or insurance coverage to pay for care, but have difficulty finding care which deals with them as whole people rather than as cardiac or kidney or gynecologic problems. A generation ago over half of all practicing physicians were general practitioners, while now the proportion is only one out of seven.[5]

People in rural areas often have great difficulty finding health care. The rural poor are especially hard hit. The most desperate are the one million American migrant workers and their families. Their living conditions are horrendous. Whole families live in one-room shacks, many with no refrigerators or screens, and as many as 25 families may share a single outhouse. The rate of infectious disease in this group is 260 percent higher than the national average, and the death rate 125 percent higher. Almost none of them are covered by health insurance of any kind, and they earn between $10 and $20 per week, barely enough many times to pay for one visit to a doctor.[6] Even rural communities that are not necessarily poor have problems with access to care. Some 5,000 of them have no physician at all.[7] Nurse practitioners are beginning to help fill this gap and undoubtedly will fill much more of it.

The recently enacted Rural Health Clinics Act authorizes payment of nurse practitioners and physicians' assistants under Medicare and Medicaid for services provided in rural clinics which meet certain health standards. Previously these individuals could be reimbursed only for services performed while a physician was present.[8]

Perhaps this will stimulate greater recognition of nurse practitioners as providers of primary care. Such recognition has been slow to develop in many rural areas. The National Health Service Corps, set up to finance the services of health care professionals in communities where the need for these services can be proven, recruits qualified professionals to fill the needs of qualifying communities. There have been few requests for nurse practitioners, and, therefore, few have been recruited into this service. Most Americans, it seems, see the physician as the only health professional who provides primary care.[9] This is a misperception we must change as we reach out for a more active role in this area.

Besides the cost of health care and access to it, Americans are becoming increasingly concerned about the quality of that care. The bureaucratized structure in which they find themselves seeking care leaves them feeling that their care is very fragmented, that no one person is responsible for the major portion of it, and that the system is inefficient at best. Concern with the quality of care is reflected in the sharply increasing numbers of medical malpractice suits being filed. Additionally, it is pointed out often and publicly that all the increased spending for health care has not necessarily improved the nation's health. The principal causes of death are still heart disease, cancer and stroke, and mortality is significantly related to preventable causes that are not generally the kind lending themselves to medical "cure." Many of these causes appear rooted in different life-styles of individuals, and unrelated to the amounts or kinds of medical care they receive. Documentation of the relationship among death rates, health status and life-style is accumulating at a rapid rate.[10] Probably the greatest potential for improving the health of the American people lies not in expanding the number of hospital beds and the amount of health care expenditures, but in teaching and motivating people to lead healthier lives.[11]

ENTER NURSING

Nurses have provided health teaching to patients on a formal and informal basis for as long as the discipline has existed, and educational programs aimed at preventing illness have been carried out by them in almost every setting in which they have worked. Because of our knowledge of health and illness and our constant contact with patients, families and others, we are the health professionals best equipped to provide continuing leadership in health education. Indeed, many of our Nurse Practice Acts explicitly make health education part of our job responsibility. As the country shifts its emphasis from medical care to health care and from the treatment of illness to the maintenance of health, some believe we are entering an "age of nursing."[12] Functions that have traditionally belonged to nursing are becoming more and more significant in the emerging health care delivery system.

Unfortunately, this does not mean that nursing suddenly will become more visible and better rewarded. It does not even mean that nursing necessarily will have a greater voice in shaping health policy. The National Health Planning and Resources Development Act, P.L.93-641, has established regional planning and coordinating bodies called Health Systems Agencies (HSAs) to grapple with the fundamental problems of health care and to guide the transition to a more health-oriented, preventive approach.[13] The law requires that nurses be appointed to the governing bodies of the HSAs, but does not necessarily ensure that their representation will be effective. Nor could any law guarantee that nurses will be heard in all the other local, state and national arenas in which public and private decisions will determine the future course of health care, or the roles of different practitioners. There are many other groups involved in health care now proclaiming as theirs what nursing has been doing for over a century. If we do not work to ensure that our voice is heard effectively, we can surrender the lead to these groups, often less capable than we, and thereby further fragment the care of people.

What we do with this opportunity depends upon us. Collectively and individually, we have been sensitized every day to the needs of the people for whom we care—the man with diabetes, discharged before he fully understands his diet; the woman with a new colostomy, discharged before she has yet learned to irrigate it; pregnant women, only half of whom we have the time to teach about pregnancy and childbirth, let alone parenting.

For too long we have become exhausted and given up in our attempts to "change the system" to meet these people's needs. Finally the government has begun to understand and deal with the problem, the public is becoming increasingly alarmed, and the system is beginning to change. Our own profession is now more mature, and we also are acknowledging openly our own feelings that we have worked too hard and too long for too little—too little recognition of our contribution, too little opportunity to use all of our ability in giving health care, too little of the power in deciding the direction of health care, and too little of the rewards. We cannot and we must not let this opportunity pass us by. To take full advantage of it, however, we must deal with a number of problems that have impeded us—problems of self-worth, of not always working together, and of not making others aware of our ability. These problems challenge each of us, and for many of us will require a resocialization in our everyday practice.

UNRESOLVED PROFESSIONAL PROBLEMS

We Do Not Accept Our Own Worth

Of the problems we face as professionals, the lingering problem of self-worth is perhaps most basic. We have inherited the problem to a large extent simply because we are a profession consisting of approximately 98 percent women.

Socialization into a Role Every society operates by established sets of values, including cultural norms or behaviors believed appropriate for individuals according to their sex. Each society uses its major institutions to reinforce the behavioral norms it has established, and changes them only as the needs of society change. Down through the ages behavior considered appropriate for women has revolved around reproduction, which has been assumed to be central in a woman's life. Medicine as well as other disciplines and institutions have been used to give the color of "science" to societal views of the behaviors appropriate for women. In much of psychiatry, women have been viewed, in the words of one author, as essentially "breeders and bearers—potentially warm-hearted creatures but primarily simple cranky children with uteri, forever mourning the loss of male organs and male identity." [14]

Sigmund Freud's influence on attitudes about the place of women in society was dominant in the 1930s. His theories of personality development tend to deny women individual identities. His concepts of castration complex and penis envy assume that women are biologically inferior to men. Freud believed that the motivating force of a woman's personality was her wish for a penis. Freud's followers further developed a concept of femininity which considered women to be passive, unstable, weak, intuitive, inconsistent, dependent, empathetic, sensitive, and subjective. By contrast, they saw men as aggressive, independent, competitive, task-oriented, stoic, analytical, rational, self-disciplined, confident, able in leadership, objective, emotionally controlled and outward-oriented.

While some of the characteristics attributed to women have positive connotations, most are traits viewed negatively in our society. The traits attributed to men, however, are ones which are strongly valued in American society—at least as long as they are possessed by men. Women who have tried to emulate some of the male characteristics, who have deviated from passive roles of wife, mother and noncompetitor and who have attempted to function in roles traditionally considered to be male, have been regarded not only as abnormal, but also as unhealthy.

The sex-appropriate behaviors supported by popular scientific thought were used as the basis for developing different educational programs for the sexes, for career counseling and for determining areas of employment. They are still reinforced in children's books, textbooks, radio and television commercials, newspaper and magazine advertisements. Through these media children learn early what behaviors are expected of them, and they have these behaviors reinforced in their everyday lives. Boys are pressured early to assume an aggressive behavior "characteristic" of their sex, but inappropriate for girls.

Kohn notes that the behavior of boys also depends on social status.[15] Boys of upper social classes are taught self-reliance, that their actions and decisions can make a difference and that they can control their fates. They are taught to be self-directed and open-minded, to trust others, to act on the basis of their own judgment and to hold personally responsible moral standards. Boys of lower classes are taught obedience. They are taught to follow the dictates of authority, to be intolerant of nonconformity and dissent, to be distrustful of others, and to have moral standards that strongly emphasize obedience to the letter of the law. In a cross-cultural study, Barry, et al. found greater social pressures for self-reliance and achievement in males generally and pressures toward nurturance, responsibility and obedience in girls.[16] Reiss, noting the parallel between values taught lower-class males in our society and those taught to females in all societies, concludes that both these groups are at a disadvantage in the occupational world because their rearing emphasizes obedience rather than self-reliance.[17]

While girls are being socialized into traditionally female roles and personalities, they also are being taught to achieve academic success in school, and, until puberty, they actually excel academically. At puberty, however, the requirements of "femininity" and normality shift toward the stereotype of female adulthood. The pressures that reinforced girls' academic achievement now work to enforce their preparation for the traditional female role.[18] Success now entails becoming a good wife and mother. Boys are socialized toward marriage also, but there is an important difference—no young man considers marriage to be his fundamental project in life.[19]

For women who choose a career, the pressure for role-appropriate behaviors remains. For many, the career can be a stopgap until marriage. Women who seriously pursue a career commonly find their femininity called into question; they are seen as possessing "masculine" characteristics of aggressiveness, achievement, motivation, independence and so on. Many find this pressure too great and adjust their career goals in line with more appropriately female occupations.

Career women who surmount these psychological hurdles find themselves facing discrimination in hiring, promotion and equal salary for equal work. Often these problems are reinforced by women themselves based on years of socialization. When men and women are given tasks to perform, men predict higher performance for themselves and evaluate their performance more favorably than do women, even when the results show that both sexes have performed equally well. Men attribute their success to their ability, women to luck. Following failure, women rate their performance more negatively than do males.[20] This behavior can only underscore the "scientific" beliefs of male superiority, as viewed by those who have the power to hire, promote and fire.

For career women who marry, the major management of the household and children is still assumed to be their function in addition to their careers. However, other studies indicate that the greater the education and professional preparation of women, the lower their divorce rate and the greater their sexual happiness in marriage.[21]

The laws of "appropriate" feminine behavior dictate that some women who succeed pay dearly for their success. Novelist Erica Jong notes that "every woman who has ever excelled in her field also knows that the bitterest experience of all is the lack of support, the envy, the bitterness we frequently get from our female colleagues. We are hard on ourselves and hard on each other, and women not only hold support from other women, they openly attack. We have too little charity for each other's work, and are too apt to let the male establishment pit us against each other."[22] On the last point, how little has changed—Florence Nightingale had to deal with the same problem among the nurses in the Crimea!

Jong and others comment on what occurs to a successful woman in a male-dominated field. She is isolated from other women since she has less in common with them, and, therefore, she receives less support and acceptance. She has had to meet higher standards than most men in the same field, and so she is rare and special, and she enjoys her position. She also will defend it vigorously, however, attacking any other woman who is seen as threatening to her special spot.[23]

The pressures experienced by career women in general are found, often exaggerated, in nursing, although they make take a slightly different form. Beginning a nursing career generally has not carried the connotation of entering a man's domain. For the most part it has been seen as an extension of the natural nurturing characteristics of women—skills that could be developed further until a woman married. Ehrenreich and English note that "the initial emphasis was on training persons in character rather than skills, to bring the wifely quality of obedience into her relationship with the physician and the selfless devotion of a mother to her patient."[24] Basically nursing continued to reinforce the previous socialization of women.

We have been under tremendous pressures to continue in that socialization. Our work places us in close contact with the very professions whose views are popularly used to give the "scientific" stamp to appropriate sex role behaviors and to the theory of female biological inferiority. As recently as 1970, a study asking 79 clinicians (psychiatrists, psychologists and social workers) to rate personality and behavioral attributes on a scale indicating degree of health for males and females came up with the same old sex role stereotypes. Males were ranked as aggressive, dominant and so on, but these characteristics were seen as reflecting pathology for the female. Females were seen as passive, dependent, and so on, in their healthy state, while for males this behavior was pathologic.[25]

This continued sex role stereotype has presented obvious barriers which prevent men from entering the profession. Men find overt pressures dissuading them from nursing, most coming from parents and often the strongest coming from fathers. Likewise, in crossing the sex boundary in occupation, they risk being typed as homosexuals. Men who do enter nursing as a career generally view themselves as pioneers or innovators; they believe their sex will be an advantage because others in the profession expect them to be leaders, administrators and change agents.[26] This continued pattern of sex stereotyping can leave both sexes feeling "used," and create even more problems within the profession if we look to others because of their sex rather than their abilities or needs.

Scully and Bart carried out a systematic review of the 27 most widely used gynecology texts published since 1943 and found continued reinforcement of stereotyped roles for women.[27] They cited the following as not atypical: "The fundamental biologic factor in women is the urge of motherhood balanced by the fact that sexual pleasure is entirely secondary or even absent."[28] In eight texts published since 1960 they found claims that the male sex drive is inherently stronger than the female, and, in six, assertions that procreation is the primary function of woman. All this after research of Kinsey and of Masters and Johnson! Personalities of men and women are similarly portrayed; for example, "An important feature of sex desire in the man is the urge to dominate woman and subjugate her to his will; in the woman acquiescence to the masterful takes a high place."[29]

A passive, dependent nurse who conforms to the behaviors appropriate for her sex and who functions without rocking the boat is indeed accepted easily within the traditional framework of health care. If, however, she sees a better way, or wants more responsibility and authority and pursues it, she is likely to be put back into her place by authorities whose attitudes parallel the following from Dr. Benjamin Spock: "Women are usually more patient in working at unexciting repetitive tasks . . . Women on the average have more passivity in the inborn core of the personality . . . I believe women are designed in their deepest instincts to get more pleasure out of life . . . not only sexually but socially, occupationally, maternally . . . when they are not aggressive. To put it another way, I think that when women are encouraged to be competitive too many of them become disagreeable."[30]

Faced with these pressures from very powerful people and groups in the everyday work setting, it becomes very difficult to function consistently in anything but the expected role. The nurse who assumes a more assertive role by questioning the status quo or by attempting to change the system commonly encounters, among other problems, the physician who tells her to get back in line—or who asks the director of nursing to tell her for him.

Just as the young girl in school is allowed to compete and excel academically until puberty, we as nurses are allowed to develop our skills and demonstrate our abilities up to a point. There are areas in which our knowledge and skills commonly equal or excel the physician's, but where we are not supposed to use them because doctors see them as medical prerogatives. Physicians continue to order nurses not to "interfere" in teaching patients about their illnesses, diets and self-care. Teaching is not reserved to medical practice by law, and in fact is assigned to nurses by many practice acts, but its arbitrary handling by many physicians only reinforces nurses' low self-esteem.

Low Salary Individuals' worth in our society also is commonly recognized by the money they receive for services. Nurses, functioning passively and dependently, have been traditionally underpaid. We have been bought off with what Galbraith refers to as "covenient social virtue." This phenomenon gives merit to any pattern of behavior, no matter how uncomfortable or unnatural for the individual involved, that serves the comfort and well-being of more powerful members of the community. The approval of the community becomes a substitute for hard cash, at least in the eyes of the community. As Galbraith notes, "such merit was never deemed a wholly satisfactory substitute for remuneration in the case of physicians."[31]

Other reasons can be cited for our low pay—for example, the lack of mobility of married women to look for higher paying jobs and the pressure on the health care industry to keep costs down. Several management authorities have another interesting theory—nursing salaries are low because nurses have failed to insist that they be paid more.[32] Another investigator concluded, "The best assessment the administrators could offer was that the treatment of nurses had remained traditional, despite substantial changes in the nursing function. As long as the nurses accepted that treatment, there was no pressure to change it."[33] We are in a vicious circle—our low pay reinforces our low sense of worth, and our low self-worth discourages us from seeking higher pay.

When we do insist on higher salaries, we are too often quoted figures purporting to demonstrate the already high cost of nursing services in the institution. As Princeton politics professor Herman Somers asked at the 1977 NLN convention, "When will nursing reply to the statement continually made that labor costs represent two thirds to three fourths of hospital costs?" In fact, he noted that labor costs as a proportion have gone down every year for the last decade and are now at 53 percent. Nursing salaries as a percentage of hospital salaries were less than 34 percent in 1976 and have declined every year since 1969.[34]

What so often happens is that our salaries are lumped with all types of other costs into a room rate which is then labeled nursing costs. If we want better pay we are accused of driving up the costs of hospitalization and are told that there is no more money. Yet, as ANA president Anne Zimmerman has noted, if a hospital is being built and the cement workers go on strike somehow the money is found.[35] We are underpaid in independent settings, too; nurse practitioners earn an average of $14,000, barely more than salaried nurses. And nurse practitioners work hours similar to those of private physicians, whose earnings average $58,000.[36]

The multitude of problems nurses face first as working women and second as women in a predominately female profession have been too much to deal with on a daily basis, and many of us have chosen to conform to the traditional role of women nurses. One of the effects is that we tend to think we are powerless. We often see ourselves as objects of the power of others and we internalize the attitudes of subordination projected by those in authority and by other health professionals. Lewis notes that there are still a lot of nurses who are happy to leave the judgmental interventions and decision making, even in nursing matters, to someone else.[37]

When people lack power and control over much of their lives, they often exercise a sense of power by controlling the behavior of others in their same position. In nursing this is often done by controlling the dress and behavior of the peer group. As a group we are competitive, but unlike other groups that compete in the outside world for money, status and power, we compete with each other and tend to withhold support from those within our ranks who show signs of succeeding.

All of these factors—passive, dependent functioning, inability to use all of our knowledge and skills, attributing successful performance to luck, being very negative when we fail, low pay, feelings of powerlessness and competition in the wrong arena—all diminish our sense of worth and leave us with a negative self-image. How do we turn it around? We all have to begin by examining ourselves and our own situations.

Evaluate Yourself Examine the setting in which you are working or being educated. What is the value system that operates? What rewards are offered for what behaviors? What items appear on your evaluation forms? Are you being socialized into dependent, passive functioning, or functioning that encourages decision making, accountability, responsibility, independence? Examine your own functioning; are you functioning passively and dependently, or more actively and independently? In which role are you more comfortable and why?

Next, list ten abilities and strengths you have. Are you using them? Does your work or educational environment make use of them and allow and encourage you to build on them? Are other people in that setting aware of your strengths? Have you told anyone about them?

Identify the last time you performed successfully. Did you feel your success was due to your ability? Did you tell others about it? What about the last time you failed at a task? Did you feel your failure was due to your inability? Did you share your failure with others? Did they support you through it?

What is your salary? Do you feel it reflects your responsibilities, performance and worth? Is it comparable to other groups of workers within your salary system who have the same education, experiential qualifications and similar levels of responsibility?

Identify the last time you felt powerless. Who or what was more powerful? Why did you need the power? What stood in the way of your getting that power?

Identify the last time someone working or studying with you was very successful at something. How did you feel? What did you feel? Did you congratulate her? What did you say to her? In what way did you support her?

Identify the last time someone with whom you were working failed at something. How did you feel? What did you feel? What did you say to her? How did you support her?

When you complete this exercise you should have an idea of the areas you can work on to increase your own sense of worth and how you can help enhance that of others. However, many of these areas require the support of others in nursing.

Turning It Around Educators can develop a positive self-image in students by providing them with the theory and practical experiences which encourage more independent functions and by allowing students to see themselves in a professional role providing a unique and essential service to society. All nursing students should have a broad-based education that builds their self-confidence by helping them to identify their abilities and to build upon them. Students should develop their speaking and writing abilities, be encouraged to be creative, to take risks, to make their own decisions and to assume accountability and responsibility for the decisions they make. They should be provided with a knowledge of how the health care delivery system works, nursing's contribution to health care, leadership theory, change process, research, basic economics, and a core of nursing knowledge and technical skills that will allow them to feel confident in giving direct patient care.

During their education they need positive reinforcement and successes and, when they fail, opportunity to learn from the experience rather than being squelched because of it. They need to be exposed to good role models in nursing. They should be exposed to nurses working in expanded roles and leadership roles, nurses doing research, those active in politics and those in hospital units and other agencies who are competent, secure practitioners. They need to be exposed to nurses who are committed to their career as well as their family, to learn these nurses' reasons for feeling as they do, and to be able to discuss ways of handling both career and family. Students also should be actively involved in peer review and in developing standards for quality assurance.

The RN student returning for higher education has special needs. We need to help these students identify their areas of expertise and strengths and help them build upon these without having to repeat experiences they already have had and mastered. Additionally, it is critical that their strengths be *recognized* and that their egos be supported rather than deflated because they "chose the wrong educational system." As never before, we need to recognize the strengths we each possess.

The list of goals may sound utopian and unrealistic for many, but for many others it is being implemented. There are many creative ways of approaching and accomplishing these goals. For example, students in a course in nursing trends might independently choose an area such as politics and spend the first half of their total class hours actively involved with a nurse who works in this area or with political candidates learning their perceptions and views of nursing and health care issues. The second half of the class hours could be used to bring students together to present what they had learned about politics, economic security, expanded roles, nursing research, or whatever area they had explored.

In the practice setting, nurses might help each other develop more positive images by developing self-help groups which focus on growth and interpersonal development. They could meet monthly in much the same manner as Thank-God-It's-Friday parties. Individual group members might begin by identifying their areas of strength, for example, technical skills, communication skills, decision making skills. From the list, a buddy system might be developed in which individuals could work together to gain from one another and to improve in areas where they do not feel secure. This group also could be used to help members who are about to embark on new phases of their careers; individuals returning to school, beginning a research project or writing a paper could gain from experiences of other members who already have gone that route. It could also function as a support group to allow for the informal sharing of group problems on the unit and in agencies or for faculties in a school.

The buddy system also could be used for new faculty, for new graduates, or for practitioners returning to health care settings after a period of time to help them get settled.

Nurse-patient contracts are another way to sharpen our sense of professional responsibility and worth. Nurses functioning in primary care may sign contracts with patients agreeing on the expectations each places on the other. The agreement identifies the nurse as the patient's resource person and advocate. This contract provides a new kind of accountability and responsibility within the setting; moreover, it gives a special kind of positive recognition to the nursing role in primary care. It can help nurses to function consistently as—and be viewed as—first-class professionals.

Likewise, each nurse could establish quarterly goals with her immediate supervisor to improve some aspect of patient care or improve functioning on the unit. When each goal is reached, the nurse should receive some form of recognition. In that same vein each nurse could be encouraged to write career goals on an annual basis. Where do *you* expect to be in five or ten years? The nurse could then be encouraged to plan for moving toward these goals, and provided with environmental support (tuition reimbursement, support of staff for innovation, and so on) to help her, and to foster her career commitment.

Many of the things we can do to increase our professional self-esteem require us to work together. Unfortunately, this has been a problem for us for many years. And yet, if consumers can get it together to achieve their goals, and if other professions can get it together to achieve their goals, why can't we more effectively pull together?

The Need to Heal Our Divisions

There are many ways in which we could better pool our efforts to become more effective. Let us begin with a continuing problem identified again in the authors' survey—that of the cliché-ridden split between service and education.

Nursing educators are often accused of graduating students who do not have adequate technical skills to perform direct care. The new graduates also supposedly are not able to take responsibility or to make decisions. Often the faultfinding becomes more heated and personal and educators are accused of not being able to practice ("that's why they went into teaching"), of being unrealistic, of expecting people in service to teach the new graduate to give actual nursing care during orientation.

On the other side of the coin, nursing service personnel are accused of focusing only on technical skills as indicators of nurses' performance, and of expecting new graduates to function at the same level as staff who have worked a year or more. They also are chided that new graduates are prepared for beginning levels of practice, not for assuming head nurse duties two weeks after they join the staff. As the criticism on this side becomes more heated, service personnel often are accused of being rigid people and of creating stifling work situations where creativity and innovation are squelched.

Because there has been so much discussion about the division for so long, one begins to wonder if each side *prefers* not to work on the problem more vigorously. Could it be that the divisions between service and education create a support base for nurses on each side? If so, it is time we directed those energies more profitably toward the greater issues we face as a profession.

In some situations dual appointment has had a beneficial effect on bringing service and education together. By working 50 percent of the time in education and 50 percent of the time in service, for example, a nurse is able to develop objectivity to the problems we all face. One nurse reports the position allows her to maintain clinical expertise while gaining knowledge and being stimulated by association with nurse educators.[38]

Where this is not practical, we could spend time working with each other. Nursing faculty could begin by spending several days working with a head nurse, and vice versa. After this *beginning*, we could establish a routine in which we maintain ongoing working relationships, legitimized by administrations in both institutions. Of course, we can think of many reasons why it could not work, but think of the benefits. To begin with, we would get to know each other better. We could identify resources we each have that could benefit the other and cut in half the energy spent in some of our efforts. We could get a better understanding of each other's problems, and we would probably begin to see that many of our problems, as well as goals, are common. We might even begin to see humor in some of our attempts to solve our problems: the instructor who smilingly and sweetly, but nevertheless routinely, palpates the bladders of all newly delivered mothers in order not to graduate any students who "haven't ever catheterized a patient"; the head nurse who smilingly attempts to pour medications from the medicine cart for twenty patients while ten students attempt to do likewise for each of their two patients. For each of us, nursing does have its moments!

The development of internship programs has helped some institutions assist young graduates in improving their skills. If lack of technical skills presents a continuing problem in the service setting why shouldn't a job applicant be evaluated on a core of technical skills prior to being hired? The new graduates should know which skills will be tested when they apply. The evaluation might be done by inservice personnel or by staff in the area to which the applicant hopes to be assigned. The evaluators will get not only a picture of the applicants' skills, but information on which to base further orientation planning. At the least, if successful testing on core skills is a prerequisite for employment, the inservice personnel will be able to pass over those areas in planning orientation. Most educators would welcome a list of skills identified by service personnel as basic to nursing, to compare with their own lists. The testing might help schools to identify possible weaknesses in their curricula.

The new staff nurse also should know what areas will be evaluated in the future, and when. All staff members, new as well as more experienced, should have an opportunity annually to evaluate their ability to practice professionally in their work environment. In some places this is now done routinely.

Through the collaborative efforts of educators and service people, we could greatly expand nursing research and improve the documentation of our practice base. A nurse who has been in practice for years has developed skills that are not found in our nursing texts; yet too often she hesitates to write about them because she feels she can't write. By getting together with someone who has these skills, perhaps an educator, these nurses could significantly augment our documented nursing practice base. As a profession, nursing cannot afford to lose the very valuable skills possessed by these experienced practitioners.

Many educators who are interested in clinical research have the talents to define and research the problem, set up the study and seek funding for it, but lack the time for data collection. They might team up with nurses already working in the settings where the data would be collected to get the research done. By complementing each other's abilities and opportunities we could do so much more.

Collaboration also would help us to avoid a trap into which we continually seem to fall. Not too many years ago, "Supernurse" was the nurse who was able to care for all of her assigned patients, pass out medications, take off orders, serve the dinner trays, run things to the laboratory and diet kitchen and back, pass out the linen, dust the patients' rooms and put away the supplies—all in zip time. "Normal nurse" rebelled against doing the work of the laboratory, the dietary department, the housekeeping department and the laundry in addition to her own. Today in our eagerness to elevate our professional status we have had a tendency to resurrect "Supernurse"; only now she must seek higher and higher degrees, be an expert practitioner, an expert teacher, an administrator, a researcher and an author as well. The goals of increasing our theory and practice base through research, increasing the educational base of our practitioners, and developing our power base so that nursing is better able to direct health care delivery and reap some of the rewards are essential to our profession, but even Florence Nightingale in all her glory could not do them all simultaneously! Yet this is often what we expect, or what is expected of us.

A typical nursing faculty member is required to conduct formal classes and supervise clinical laboratory experience, counsel students, develop program evaluation tools, take part in several committees, keep abreast of trends in health care and new learning and teaching methods, maintain good relationships with numerous outside groups, monitor the professional and personal growth of students, meet professional standards for both nursing and teaching, assume responsibility for personal and professional growth, take part in professional and community activities, and conduct nursing research and publish the results.

Nurses working in direct care are under the same kinds of pressures to develop expertise in practice, deal with standards of care and quality assurance, advance their formal education, and conduct research. Many of the areas overlap and in others we could help each other tremendously. Instead of each group trying to invent the wheel, by working together we could create the wheels and the cart and have secured funding for an animal to pull it!

We should not focus our efforts solely on collaboration between education and service. Within each arena there are many ways we could pool resources and expand our services. In education there could be much more sharing of learning laboratory facilities and of all types of equipment. There could be much more exchange of faculty for periods of time to stimulate new ideas and develop new perspectives. There could be many more shared student learning experiences between schools. It could only enhance students' learning to have an elective in a setting very different from that in which the program is located. We could also build more shared learning experiences between graduate and undergraduate students. This could help foster collegial relationships, allow undergraduates to hear more about graduate education, and expose them to a broader range of perspectives. It would also help to develop the "old girl system" in nursing.

In service areas the same exchanges could be used for many of the same reasons. Clinical specialists, or other members of the staff, might be exchanged for periods of time to bring back new ideas and perspectives. There might be much more sharing of inservice educational experiences among institutions. This sharing would help us to develop better collegial relationships and would encourage us to call upon one another for advice with clinical problems as other disciplines do. In both education and service those of us with more experience could and should serve as mentors for those with less. Had we been doing more of this we would undoubtedly have less of a leadership crisis at present.

It is especially important to work together on basic issues that deal with powers outside the profession—our economic security and the conditions under which we practice. As Rebecca Clark Culpepper, former executive director of the Tennessee State Nurses' Association observed, "nurses never could have gotten the Memphis-Shelby County Hospital Authority even to bargain with them—much less to give significant increases in pay and to agree to major quality assurance gains—if they had not been determined to remain united."[39] As pressures grow to control health care costs, some inevitably will seek to cut costs by compromising nursing care standards. We need our unity now more than ever.

Our Image with Others

A crucial third step in reaching our goals is to make others aware of our abilities, namely powers such as health care administrators, physicians and other health care workers, legislators and the general public. Recently a nursing leader was quoted as saying that nursing's image will not be helped by a Madison Avenue approach but rather by a word-of-mouth, one-to-one sharing. While the latter is certainly necessary, why, one would ask, would the former approach be so successful for medicine and other groups and not for nurses? Television certainly has stereotyped the role of the nurse and in many instances left us with a negative image. Since this medium alone reaches millions of viewers, think of how many mouths and one-to-one sharings we would have to stimulate in order to undo the effects of just one night's viewing. We have been sitting in the corner too long waiting to be discovered; it is time we took our own act on the road. If we cannot sell ourselves and our services, who will do it for us?

Political Image Legislators are key people in the power structure who must be educated to nursing and its contribution to health care delivery. Nurses represent one powerful voting bloc. While smaller power groups may have more money to spend, nurses have the advantage of potentially influencing nearly a million votes. On the national and on the state levels there is much movement in the political arena. The ANA has lobbyists in Washington explaining nursing and nursing's position to congressmen and their staffs, to decision makers in the administration and to many legislative committees.

In 1971, a group of nurses in New York asked the ANA to do more to make nurses more effective in politics. When the ANA did not immediately respond, they set up an organization of their own and attempted to get into politics. Later, the ANA supported the effort and created the first nurses' political action committee, the Nurses Coalition for Action in Politics (NCAP). The group made its first political contributions in the 1976 congressional races, contributing small amounts to 95 candidates and endorsing 189 congressional candidates with a letter. More than 90 percent of those endorsed and 80 percent of those to whom money was sent were elected.[40]

In a recent editorial on political imperatives in the *American Journal of Nursing,* Schorr notes a number of goals toward which we need to continue to direct our energies in the political arena:

1. An authoritative nursing voice at the decision-making level in the formation of national health policy.
2. Recognition that health care is more than medical care, and that medical and nursing care are two distinct entities.
3. Reimbursement for nursing services as nursing services, not as part of a catch-all bed-and-board hospital price that gets inflated by a variety of other costs and is misrepresented to patients as "nursing" costs.
4. Federal funding for nursing research.
5. Funding for nursing education.
6. Ratification of the Equal Rights Amendment to equalize opportunities and protect human rights for all people.[41]

The NLN also works in the national political arena. In addition to providing testimony on health care issues and presenting its views to congressmen, consumers and organized groups, it sponsors a program of summer study fellowships in public policy. The project was established in 1975 in an attempt to forge a link between policymakers and potential nursing leaders. Selected nursing students are assigned for nine weeks in the U.S. Department of Health, Education and Welfare and in congressional offices. Under the guidance of governmental staff preceptors, all are actively involved in the policymaking process: analyzing bills, developing proposals, researching issues and writing reports.

Before the program was established, no congressional office with health policy input had employed a nurse or a nursing student in a professional staff capacity. Since then four NLN fellows have been retained for staff assignments in congressional offices. Other former fellows are involved in state and local HSAs and PSROs, and as nursing-community contacts for congressional offices.[42] The NLN also has sponsored seminars to help faculty become more knowledgeable about the politics and legislation on health care issues.

Nurses are increasingly being called upon for their input into legislation and to testify in committee hearings. The presence of Ingeborg Mauksch on the Advisory Committee on National Health Insurance Issues of the Department of Health, Education and Welfare testifies not only to her individual abilities, but to the work of many to secure more nursing representation on national policy and decision-making levels.

At the state and local levels, there are varying degrees of political activity. Let us assess political activity at the local level. Have you voted in the last election? Who is your local representative, your state representative? What state bills and national legislation regarding health care are pending? If you do not know, pick up your telephone and call your district nurses' association; see how long it takes to find out. Perhaps they could use your help. When you find out, what effect will that legislation have on health care and on your own practice? When you go to work tomorrow, ask your colleagues these same questions. Do they know the answers? If not, if many of us are uninformed, what impact can we hope to have on legislation? If nurses in practice are really concerned about the delivery of health care, are we concerned enough to slip current legislative affairs into shift reports once a month, or into head nurse meetings or inservice meetings? If faculties are to produce students who are politically aware, can they do this without being up-to-date themselves? Are they willing to slip a brief report on legislative matters into faculty meetings or report on current legislation in each course, rather than leaving it all for trends in nursing where it will be seen as something outside everyday nursing practice?

To keep ourselves informed as a group, we should include brief legislative reports during programs on continuing education and at dinner meetings of local nursing organizations. Our local, state and national nursing groups send out bulletins on legislative matters. This is great, but too often they are tacked to bulletin boards and forgotten. We need more of these communications, and we need them written so that they explain in nonlegalistic terms exactly what each new political development or item of pending legislation means to us and to our practice.

Another method being used locally to keep nurses informed is a special telephone number that a nurse can dial to hear a tape-recorded update on legislative issues of interest to nursing. At election times it would also be helpful to have the various candidates' stands on health care issues recorded. It would be even more helpful to invite panels of candidates to periodic dinner or luncheon meetings to present their views and to be questioned by nurses in the audience. It would also serve to inform them of the interest of nurses in health care legislation and of the group's potential voting power.

Students might also invite candidates to their schools to speak. As a group we should make certain we have nurse representation in key campaigns. We should have students involved in the process, possibly to meet a partial requirement of their trends course.

Legislators have commented on how helpful they have found

nurses in their campaigns. In the words of one candidate who succeeded with nurse backing, nurses "are accustomed to dealing with people and particularly people's problems. So they're not flabbergasted, they're not caught flat-footed, if someone brings up an issue or mentions a problem to them that the public official needs to be concerned with." He added that his nurse supporters came into his campaign "whole hog . . . all the way. They contributed personally, financially through their group organizations, and more important than money, they came in with time and effort."[43] He won the election over a physician candidate strongly backed by the state medical society.

Not only should we be supporting candidates who will work for goals similar to ours, but we should be identifying and supporting politically astute and articulate nurses to run for public office on local, state and national levels. Because of our constant exposure to the concerns of people with their everyday problems of living, we should have nurses competing for all sorts of elected and appointive positions—school boards, civic association leadership, local councils, water and sewer authorities, planning commissions, housing authorities and similar bodies, as well as for legislative and executive offices. Consider for a moment Lillian Wald's accomplishments as a member of the New York Joint Board of Sanitary Control and the Factory Visiting Committee!

Image with Physicians   Physicians and other members of the health care team are also target groups that need to be better informed about the education and contributions of nurses to overall health care delivery. Two fairly recent events should highlight this need.

In March of 1976, the report of the Commission on Physicians for the Future was issued at a press conference by the prestigious Josiah Macy Foundation, which sponsored the commission's two-year study. The commission was made up of distinguished leaders of universities and their medical centers, public representatives and authorities in medical care and medical manpower. The public representatives on the panel included the president of Cornell University, the president of Jackson State University, the president emeritus of Radcliffe College and the editor of the *Scientific American*. The report's view of the nurse's role defies belief. As reported in the *American Journal of Nursing* of April 1976, the blue-ribbon group said:

> During the past fifteen years the traditional role of the nurse increasingly changed into an administrative and supervisory one. Today, however, they are participating more and more in

medical care. As the result of in-hospital course work and on-the-job training, for example, nurses now play the major role in monitoring neonatal and intensive and coronary care units, frequently making the first intervention in an emergency.

The national effort to develop new types of health workers drew attention to the potentialities of nurses, and particularly to the contributions of nurse practitioners in *extending the traditional nursing role to include direct patient care* . . . (italics *AJN's*).[44]

The other incident occurred at the 1976 National Student Nurses' Association convention, where the topic for the keynote session was "Nursing Practice 1984—Future Shock." The shock, however, as Thelma Schorr reported, would wait for no future. The president of the American Medical Association, Max Parrott, presented a speech which left nursing ancillary to medicine, dependent and exempt from accountability. During his presentation he attacked the presentation of a medical student panelist. She had criticized her medical education as being disease-oriented rather than people-oriented and had pleaded for interdisciplinary learning that could lead to real health care teamwork because it would provide the various team members with an understanding of what the others could contribute. Apparently things went downhill further when Parrott described his relationship with the nurses he employs in his office. "I've got four girls," he said, "and they do everything. They answer the phones, they fill prescriptions . . . they are really doing medicine under my license."[45]

These two events should illustrate the crying need we have to update physicians and other powerful people to nursing's contribution and its legitimate right to be recognized for that contribution! Even when we attempt to educate some physicians they refuse. Some people attribute this problem to differences in groups regarding education, financial reward and sex, and the general tendency of the public to hold medicine in higher regard than nursing.

For many years, the educational preparation of nurses and physicians was different; today, however, there are many overlapping areas. More of nursing education is found in colleges and universities, and the educational preparation of many nurses working in extended roles in six years. Physicians prepared in accelerated programs in some medical colleges have only five-years' post high school preparation before entering practice or internship. As more nurses are prepared on the graduate and doctoral levels, the differential in education between the two groups will continue to diminish. This should eliminate the problem mentioned by Hoekelman that "people with more educational credentials tend to dominate those with less in both overt and subtle ways."[46]

Increased educational preparation should help our economic problem which directly affects how others view us. Generally income is positively correlated with educational levels. One common exception, of course, is sex differences and in this, medicine is no different from society in general.[47]

The dominant male position in health care also is accentuated by the fact that doctors often are the employers of nurses, or, if both are employees, the physician enjoys a position of hierarchical superiority. How do we remove these barriers and begin developing more collegial relationships? Schaffrath mentions that physicians and nurses generally are able to work together in real life situations, but that it is primarily in the more abstract doctor-nurse relationship that problems occur.[48]

On the National Joint Practice Commission, nurses and physicians work together on collegial terms. As we noted in the previous chapter, this group was formed in 1971 by the ANA and AMA to help improve the delivery of health care in the United States through the joint practice of nurses, physicians and other health care workers. By 1977, when the commission published its casebook, *Together*, it had developed information about more than 250 joint practices in family practice, pediatrics, obstetrics, psychiatry and other specialties across the nation in urban, suburban and rural settings. The cases illustrate different ways in which collaboration as colleagues can increase the effectiveness of both professionals' practices.[49]

Sometimes it is just a doctor and nurse sharing a professional office—but with both names on the door and a division of professional responsibilities, not as employer and employee. In one such case, the physician introduced the joint practice to his patients with a letter stating: "Joining me in the office will be_____, RN......Because of our collegial teamwork, we will be more available for patient care._____ will be providing any nursing care needed and, in addition, will be available for physical examinations, treatment of minor illness and chronic disease, as well as teaching and counseling. I regularly confer with her regarding patient care and management. I hope you will ask for her, particularly when I am not available. We are a 'first' . . . team of medicine and nursing private practitioners."

Often cases are highly varied. In an inner city hospital, a nurse may provide primary care in collaboration with the physicians who come and go on various training rotations; and it is the nurse who provides continuity and the touch of human relationship that makes the care superior. In a rural mountain setting or an urban neighborhood, a nurse practitioner may run an outreach clinic in close, collegial collaboration with physicians in a hospital or central clinic two miles—or 25 miles—away. In whatever settings, joint practices have generated new types of patient-nurse-doctor relationships that have proved satisfactory to all three. Reviewing the cases, former ANA president Rosamond C. Gabrielson concluded that it was clear that "when a physician and nurse enter into joint practice, a broader spectrum of health services is made available to the consumer."[50]

Collegial relationships can also be fostered by having nursing and medical students educated together. Many areas, such as history taking, physical examinations, analysis of health care delivery and so on can be taught to students of both disciplines. Some schools also combine the medical students and nursing students in home visiting experiences and clinical rotations. Wherever this is attempted, it requires doctors and nurses who are committed to an interdisciplinary approach and who have respect for each other's role; otherwise, students are socialized into the same old hierarchical role relationships. In many of these situations it is helpful for the nursing students to be graduate students who are on a similar educational level as the medical students. There is less tendency then for the nursing student to be in awe of the older, more educated medical student. Where joint educational opportunities are limited, nursing students should still be exposed, as part of their clinical experience, to settings in which joint practices and collegial relationships are working.

Interdisciplinary education often involves the case study approach to patient care; here, each discipline is able to present its approach and contribution to care. A similar approach can be used in inservice settings where nurses and physicians are interested in fostering a collegial approach to care.

Collegial relationships and interdisciplinary approaches to patient care can also be explored in inservice programs through the use of a series of taped interviews with groups of health care workers who practice collegially. Such a series might be presented weekly, featuring teams, perhaps from rehabilitation, psychiatry or other clinical specialties, discussing the advantages and disadvantages of the team method for both patients and team members. The final presentation could feature the traditional approach, with all of the health team members again commenting on the advantages and disadvantages of that approach. There should be question or discussion periods at the end of each session, especially the last. The entire series should have a catchy title, depending on the particular institution and its problems.

Nurses who identify community needs might also form interdisciplinary groups to attempt to meet these needs and thus build interdisciplinary approaches under their own leadership. Other ways of developing collegial relationships are for nurses to function as colleagues on university, hospital and agency committees, as well as on HSAs and PSRO committees. We must not only be visible on these committees, but make sure that we function there as colleagues of other members.

Lastly, we can only function as colleagues with members of other disciplines as we develop collegial relationships with each other. For many, this will require a reorientation. Traditional administrative structures with multiple layers of hierarchical supervisory personnel, either in service or education, foster hierarchical rather than collegial functioning. Structures in which decision making is decentralized encourage not only collegial functioning, but leadership development as well.

Image with Health Care Administrators   Our image with hospital administrators needs building. Too often they simply are not aware of our achievements—past, present and potential. When the AHA honored ten great leaders in health care, none was a nurse; similarly, when the same group of administrators recounted mileposts in the 20th century evolution of health care, none was a nursing milepost.[51] Fortunately, we have the facts on our side and we can develop the tools to make administrators more aware. Part of this, as Rotkovich suggests, is simply that the nursing director needs to continuously remind her administrator what nurses concretely do for patients. We need to keep reminding them of the comprehensiveness of the service a nurse, especially in primary care, provides each patient. We need to keep reminding them that it costs more to supervise less trained personnel than it does to pay professional nurses, and of the value in grateful patients, satisfied doctors, and low rates of costly turnover of having a nursing staff that is allowed to function at a high level of professionalism.[52]

If we devise ways to demonstrate the cost-effectiveness of good nursing to administrators convincingly—at the same time we are also convincing the outside powers who influence the flow of third-party funds into hospitals—we will find ourselves enjoying sudden new respect in administrators' eyes. To do this, we ourselves need to become more knowledgeable about health care economics.

We need more nurses with backgrounds in business and public health administration who can articulate nursing viewpoints in management's own language. We also need to learn how to enlist other powers within hospitals to work with us. And we need to learn how to build our case systematically, beginning with well-designed pilot demonstrations of hospital changes which can improve cost-effectiveness while enhancing our own practice.

Public Image The need to update our image in the public's eyes has been identified in our literature, meetings and in day-to-day conversations. We need to become more visible to the general public and to make people more aware of the variety of settings in which we give care and of the various roles nurses assume.

One of the ways we could become more visible is to identify community needs and to begin working on solutions to meeting those needs. The NLN's involvement at the national level in the drive to immunize school-age children is one example of this approach.[53] On a local level many groups of nurses—school nurses, occupational health nurses and so on—are aware of community needs or examples of serious gaps in health care. Needs may already have been identified by other community groups, but may still be awaiting action; nurses can enhance their standing and help the community by assuming leadership here, too.

As a group we could offer more of our services to various community groups. In some locales we have compiled lists of nurses who have expertise in a certain area, such as health teaching of school children, problems of adolescence, coping with problems of the golden years, first aid and so on. Such lists could be circulated more aggressively to various community groups—local clubs, the schools, scout troops, PTAs, groups of senior citizens—who often need speakers.

If hospitals or universities have speakers bureaus, nurses with special expertise or interests should be listed. Nursing students also could be involved, and often are, in teaching health care to groups of school children and adolescents, many times as partial credit for class requirements. Where health teaching to community groups has been well planned, funding should be sought to maintain the project for the community.

Another way nurses could become more visible and serve the

community is by offering to do special programs for radio geared to issues of daily living, parenting, ways to combat depression, and so on. These programs might be featured close to the holidays, for example, when the suicide rate is increased. They might call attention to times of crisis in everyone's lives and how to deal with these crises or where to get help. We could also make a strong case for presenting programs on health care issues to local television stations, or of having them do features on the role of nurses in the local area. Likewise, children's programs often run features on different occupations or features on what parents do. Programs of this nature might be featured during National Nurse Week.

This particular week also should be used to plan special programs, such as having key people in the community—perhaps even a member of the press—spend a few hours or a day with a nurse as was suggested by the ANA during the Year of the Nurse 1977–1978. National Nurse Week could also be the time to present local awards to nurses who had developed new or improved ways of delivering health or nursing care to people in the community. The award criteria might be structured so that nominees for the award had to submit data that clearly showed that their approach to care was more effective in some way, perhaps more cost-effective.

The awards themselves might be presented at a dinner where key community and political leaders could be invited to present the awards. Members of the press certainly would be invited. The occasion would underscore the contributions nurses are making, the data would be available to key community and political leaders, and it would improve the image of nursing in the community's eyes as well as giving recognition to individuals or groups of nurses for their special contributions. It should also motivate other nurses to make similar efforts.

Another way nurses can increase their visibility and make more of their knowledge available to the general public is to increase the scope of their publications. For the most part, nurses have attempted to publish in nursing and health care journals. These are important targets. More nurses should write for medical journals and journals aimed at other members of the health care team to increase communication and share their perspective with these colleagues. For college and university faculties publication in these journals is rewarded.

However, if we truly are in the business of providing a service to the general public, we should also be writing for lay publications. Magazines sold in supermarkets reach vast populations and we could accomplish a great deal of health teaching through these media. Children's magazines should be another target medium. Since publication has become more of an expectation in nursing, perhaps submission of an article to a magazine or journal should be a requirement of some course during graduate school. McCloskey recently published a very helpful article in *Nurse Educator* in which she listed 65 journals which could be targets of publication for nurses and summarized the steps to take in submitting articles.[54] For nurses interested in writing for lay magazines and book publishers, a moderately priced book called the *Writer's Market* is published annually with the same type of information.[55] It and others like it are found in the public library.

We have now looked at areas in which change has been accomplished in nursing, and we, the authors, have looked at areas we feel through our own experience and research need more work. What would you like to see changed? Fantasize for a moment, then see how much you are helping your fantasy to become reality.

List ten things you would most like to see changed in nursing.

1.
2.
3.
4.
5.
6.
7.
8.
9
10.

Now list them again in order of priority, beginning with the one you want most.

1.
2.
3.
4.
5.
6.
7.
8.
9.
10.

As your next step, put an A beside each change that can be accomplished by you alone, and a G next to each that will require group action. Lastly, date each item to indicate approximately when *you* worked on the change last.

Want to do more? Read on.

References

1. Renee C. Fox, "The Medicalization and Demedicalization of American Society." *Daedalus* (Winter 1977): 9–22.
2. Enid Nemy, "When Severe Illness Plays Havoc with Family Life." *New York Times,* August 15, 1973.
3. Herbert Klarman, "The Difference the Third Party Makes." *The Journal of Risk and Insurance* 36, 553–566 (December 1969): 554.
4. Edwin Newman, "What Price Health?" *NBC Reports,* National Broadcasting Company, December 19, 1972.
5. Victor R. Fuchs, *Who Shall Live?* New York: Basic Books, 1974, p. 68.
6. Newman, "What Price Health?"
7. Fuchs, *Who Shall Live?* p. 69.
8. "Rural Health Bill Signed: Payments to NPs Authorized." *American Journal of Nursing* 78, 1 (January 1978): 8.
9. Margaret E. Walsh, *Health Issues of Today—Perspectives of Tomorrow.* New York: National League for Nursing, 1976, p. 7.
10. Herman Somers, "Our Goal is Health, Not Medical Care." Princeton University: *A Princeton Quarterly* 65, 12 (Summer 1975).
11. Walsh, *Health Issues of Today,* p. 8.
12. *Ibid.,* p. 10.
13. Melinda M. McLemore, "Nurses as Health Planners—Our New Legal Status." *Nursing Digest* (Spring 1977): 59–60.
14. Phyllis Chesler, "Women as Psychiatric and Psychotherapeutic Patients." *Journal of Marriage and the Family* 33, 753 (November 1971).
15. Melvin L. Kohn, "Class and Conformity: An Interpretation." In Ira L. Reiss, ed., *Readings on the Family System.* New York: Holt, Rinehart and Winston, 1972, p. 331.
16. Herbert Barry, Margaret Bacon, and Irvin Child, "A Cross-Cultural Survey of Some Sex Differences in Socialization." In Reiss, *Readings on the Family System,* p. 42.
17. Reiss, *Readings on the Family System,* p. 329.
18. Judith M. Bardwick, and Elizabeth Douvan, "Ambivalence—the Socialization of Women." In Vivian Gornick and Barbara Moran, eds., *Woman in Sexist Society: Studies in Power and Powerlessness.* New York: Basic Books, 1971, p. 229.
19. Simone de Beauvoir, *The Second Sex.* New York: Vintage Books, 1974, p. 482.
20. Kay Deaux and Elizabeth Farris, "Attributing Causes for One's Own Performance: The Effects of Sex, Norms and Outcome." *Journal of Research in Personality* 11, 59–72 (November 1977): 59.

21. Judith S. Shockley, "Perspectives in Femininity." *Nursing Digest* 49–52 (November-December 1975): 51.
22. Erica Jong, "Speaking of Love." *Newsweek,* February 21, 1977, p. 11.
23. *Ibid.*
24. Barbara Ehrenreich and Deirdre English, *Witches, Midwives and Nurses: A History of Women Healers,* ed. 2. New York: The Feminist Press, 1972.
25. Broverman, et al., "Sex-Role Stereotypes and Clinical Judgments of Mental Health." *Journal of Consult. Clinical Psychology* 34, 1–7 (February 1970).
26. Patricia Bush, "The Male Nurse." *Nursing Forum* XV, 390–405 (1976): 404.
27. Diana Scully and Pauline Bart, "A Funny Thing Happened on the Way to the Orifice: Women in Gynecology Textbooks." *American Journal of Sociology* 78, 1045–1050 (January 1973).
28. W. R. Cooke, *Essentials of Gynecology.* Philadelphia: J. B. Lippincott Company, 1973, p. 59.
29. T. N. A. Jeffcoate, *Principles of Gynecology,* ed. 3. New York: Appleton-Century-Crofts, 1967, p. 726.
30. B. M. Spock, *Decent and Indecent,* rev. ed. New York: Fawcett World, 1971, pp. 32–33.
31. John Kenneth Galbraith, "The Economics of the American Housewife." *Atlantic* 232; 78–83 (August 1973): 78.
32. Marjorie Godfrey, "Someone Should Represent Nurses." *Nursing 76* 73–86 (June 1976): 79.
33. *Ibid.,* p. 81.
34. Herman Somers, "Perspectives." *NLN News* 25, 1–15 (May–June 1977): 8.
35. Diane Judge, "The New Nurse: A Sense of Duty and Destiny." *Nursing Digest* (November–December 1975): 20–24.
36. Matt Clark, Frank Maier, Phyllis Malamud, and Evert Clark, "The Supernurses." *Newsweek,* December 5, 1977, p. 64.
37. Edith P. Lewis, "We Can't Have it Both Ways." *Nursing Outlook* 25, 167 (March 1977): 167.
38. Lavaun W. Sutton, "The Clinical Nurse Specialist in a Dual Role." In Joan P. Riehl and Joan W. McVay, *The Clinical Nurse Specialist Interpretations.* New York: Appleton-Century-Crofts, 1973, pp. 222–232.
39. "Nashville Contract Includes Nursing Administrators." *American Journal of Nursing* 76, 12 (November 1976): 1730.
40. "Nurses Losing Patience." *The American Nurse* (May 15, 1977): 5.
41. Thelma Schorr, "Political Imperatives," *American Journal of Nursing* 76, 10 (October 1976): 1585.
42. "Public Policy Fellowships." *NLN News* 25, 4 (April 1977): 7.
43. Bob Gammage. Personal communication with Val Fleishackker of N-CAP Washington, D.C.
44. Thelma Schorr, "Tunnel Visionaries." *American Journal of Nursing* 76, 4 (April 1976): 559.

45. Thelma Schoor, "Current Shock." *American Journal of Nursing* 76, 6 (June 1976): 911.
46. Robert A. Hoekelman, "Nurse-Physician Relationships," *American Journal of Nursing* 75, 7 (July 1975): 1151.
47. *Ibid.*, p. 1151.
48. Judge, "The New Nurse," p. 24.
49. Berton Roueche, "Together: A Casebook of Joint Practice in Primary Care." Chicago: Educational Publications and Innovative Communications, 1977.
50. *Ibid.*, p. X.
51. Rachel Rotkovitch, "Message." *American Journal of Nursing* 76, 8 (August 1976): 1261.
52. Rachel Rotkovitch, "Internal Influences for Change in Nursing Service." In *The Future Is Now*. New York: National League for Nursing, 1974, pp. 33–39.
53. "Childhood Immunization." *NLN News* 25, 4 (April 1977): 9.
54. Joanne McCloskey, "Publishing Opportunities for Nurses: A Comparison of 65 Journals." *Nurse Educator* 2, 4 (July–August 1977): 4–12.
55. Jane Koester and Paula Sandhage, eds., "Writer's Market 77." Cincinnati: Writer's Digest, 1976.

THREE

Thinking It

We have seen in the first two chapters that many nurses have been able to bring about significant change, both in the status of nursing and in health care. We have seen that many nurses today are aggressively addressing important needs for further change.

Too often, however, we have seen the need for change only after someone else has struggled to show that it can work. Too often we have simply accepted change thrust upon us by other nurses, by doctors, by hospital administrators, by the indiscriminate rush to use new technology, and by ill-informed public officials. Historically we have reacted passively to changes that affect us, even when those changes have left us with feelings of fear, anger and frustration.

This is still true. Our nursing periodicals and newsletters, our meetings, our daily work problems, and publications such as Kramer's *Reality Shock* confirm the frustrations we experience in our everyday professional lives.[1] Why is it that we largely fail to alter this situation? Is it because, like all human beings, we are prone to shrug things off and hope for the best? Is it because we feel we are too weak to take on the powers-that-be in health care? Maybe this is part of it, but it goes beyond that; often we also fail to act decisively because we do not have the knowledge and the basic, practical skills needed to accomplish change in an environment of great social and institutional complexity.

Generally, our education has overlooked these skills. In the last few years we have seen exciting new developments in nursing education designed to provide us with tools for leading change. But these have only scratched the surface; sooner or later, we need to recognize in all of our nursing curricula, our inservice programs and our professional organizations that change skills have to be developed by intensive educational processes much like the processes we use to develop our more traditional nursing skills. Most of us have not had the benefit of this kind of education.

In this chapter we will review some of the theory of change, the types of change and basic processes of change. These concepts help us to understand, develop and effectively use the skills for making change happen.

THE NATURE OF CHANGE

When we use the term "change," we mean a process which leads to alterations in individual or institutional patterns of behavior. Change occurs constantly in all human institutions. We can categorize change in many ways. Often it is viewed only in the simplest terms, according to whether we see its effects as being good or bad. Or we may differentiate it by the degree to which we actively seek to influence its outcome. At the one extreme, if we choose not to become involved, change will occur by drift; at the other end of the scale, if we intervene according to a comprehensive strategy for change, we can achieve truly planned change. Here, of course, we are interested mainly in the theory and practice of planned change. Historically this has been the exception rather than the rule in nursing.

Change by Drift

We have already pointed out many exceptions, but as a whole we have allowed our profession and our environment to change by drift. Sometimes such a stance to change is chosen consciously; usually it is not. Change accumulates around us without our involvement, sometimes almost without our noticing.

How often have we greeted some small change in patient care, initiated by someone who does not care for patients, by tsk-tsking, "Look what that idiot has done now!" and dropped it at that? Change by drift is a process marked by this kind of passivity, by our failure to think through the consequences of many small actions, by changes that seem to come almost by happenstance; yet its results may affect us as profoundly as any planned change, and not necessarily beneficially.

Health care right now is in the grip of a dramatic change by drift—the runaway spiral of health care costs. No one planned it; yet people in the health care field have made the millions of small decisions that have added up to this disaster, and perhaps more important, these actions have been accepted passively by nearly all of us. How much sheer waste have we winked at around us? Now rising costs are creating pressures for the kind of controls that could jeopardize the independence and self-direction of the health care professions. The lesson is plain. Unless we have no personal or professional goals, change by drift has little to recommend it.

Traditional Approaches to Change

There are more active approaches which still fall short of planned change. These are sometimes lumped together as the "traditional" or "popular" approach. They tend to be ad hoc or specific in nature, and to rely on three basic elements—education, emotional arousal and coercion. Sometimes the approach is almost purely educational, based on the idea that if people are shown the facts they will choose the most logical course of action. Such an approach may take the form of a consultant study, a position paper, a "blue ribbon commission," a one-shot public relations or educational campaign. The results have not been impressive. Often such efforts result in thoroughly researched and well-reasoned reports which have very little real impact—some of the best examples in nursing are the reports on needs of nursing education which have appeared from time to time since 1900.

If the approach combines education with an emotional component, it often wins more results. Such a combination has brought stunning success in mass immunization programs, especially against poliomyelitis. In other cases where the emotional component has been less well developed, immunization programs have had less enduring success, for example, the programs against measles and other childhood ailments.

Sometimes an element of coercion is added; to carry forward the earlier example, some childhood immunization programs succeed mainly because children are required by law to attend school and must be immunized to attend. Industry often uses an approach in which a consultant is hired to make recommendations and the recommendations are then imposed by fiat. Many attempts at legislative reform have similar intent—to force the bad guys, for example polluters, to change their behavior. There is a common feature to all these traditional methods—they rely on outside expertise, superior knowledge or superior power to "sell" or force a predefined change on people.

Because the traditional approaches commonly failed, social scientists in recent years have begun to study the process of change much more systematically. Their basic finding comes as no surprise—change is a complex process, and people rarely, if ever, swallow whole a simple or singleminded approach. They react to it, resist it, subvert it, sometimes exploit it—and unless the proposal was developed with these things in mind, the result always differs from the original intent. Research shows that change cannot be pursued successfully unless the people seeking change take into account two questions: What are the relationships of people within the group, institution or "system" that need changing, and what are the relationships between the system and other systems around it? The means to answer these questions and to use the answers effectively for planning change are contained in the relatively recent theory of planned change. This theory draws its concepts from many other fields of social science—learning theory, interpersonal theory, systems theory and communication theory.

Planned Change

Planned change can be defined as a deliberate and collaborative process involving a change agent and a client system. The definition bears a closer look. It says first that the process is *deliberate;* it is based on a conscious plan which sets goals and defines how those goals can be achieved. The definition also emphasizes *collaboration;* the process must actively involve everyone concerned. The definition suggests that planned change requires a *change agent,* a professional who relies on a systematic body of knowledge about change to guide the process, who possesses interpersonal competence, and who has been given (or has assumed) a mandate to help plan and accomplish change. And finally the definition also includes, as a collaborator with the change agent, a *client system;* this may be an individual, a group of people, an agency, an organization or a social institution.

Planned change is distinguished among other things by the distribution of power. No one dictates. The change agent and the elements of the system—the people or groups within it—work out the goals and strategies together. The process is open. All who desire it receive the opportunity to define their interest in change, their expectation of how it should come out, and their views on the plan and strategy for achieving change.

Participation in planned change demands a heavy investment of individual and collective time and energy. But the rewards are commensurate. Planned change can have a unifying rather than a divisive effect on the client system. Applied within nursing, it can help the profession clarify its purposes and increase its effectiveness in seeking to improve its own status and to create a better health care system for people.

CHANGE PROCESS MODELS

Various authors have developed a number of "models" to describe the process of planned change. We will review three of these models briefly before turning to the pragmatic problem-solving model which has been advanced by several authors and which constitutes the basic approach of this book.

The model advanced by Kurt Lewin is an elaborate three-stage metaphor of unfreezing, moving and refreezing.[2] The first step, unfreezing, is described as the stage of "breaking the habit—disturbing the equilibrium." During this stage, Lewin says, the change agent may deliberately use tactics designed to raise the level of discontent and to lead the client or members of the client system to identify a discrepancy between what the client views as ideal and his actual situation. Often this step, setting the stage for change, can be accomplished only if the client or the client system perceives a major threat to the self.

Once unfreezing has succeeded, the client or client system is left with a feeling of uneasiness or a sense of disequilibrium. All is not well. There is a danger, of course, that the client will become so threatened that he will become completely defensive; if that danger is avoided the client or system will be ready to "move." In practice, he will now be ready to examine why he feels uneasy and will be open to suggestions on how to narrow the perceived gap between the ideal and the reality. The change agent works with the client to identify and eliminate barriers to change, to establish realistic goals and alternatives, and to make available the tools needed for movement. After the client has reached his goals he is helped to regain a sense of stability in the "refreezing" stage.

A simpler model is offered by Alvin Pitcher, whose basic approach consists of two elements: "You have to *push* from the bottom and *persuade* at the top."[3] Although many traditional approaches to change have relied heavily on efforts to persuade key leaders of the need for change, Pitcher argues that such efforts will be nonproductive unless they are accompanied by efforts to generate a push for change from the bottom. This principle is so widely used in present-day strategies for legislative change that it is recognized in U.S. tax laws, which draw a distinction between "lobbying," or direct efforts to persuade legislators, and "grass roots lobbying," or efforts to arouse legislators' constituents so that they will prod the legislators to act.

Sanger used the persuade-push approach to seek changes in the Comstock Act. When a woman wrote requesting birth control information, she would reply that the information would be provided gladly if the law allowed. She would add that the woman's congressman had a chance to vote for this bill, and would instruct her how to write to this legislator. Sanger would make it even easier by enclosing a stamped envelope addressed to the congressman. At the same time, she and her allies were working to persuade the legislators from the top.

Seifert and Clinebell offer a third model for planned change. It has five steps: (1) motivation and preparation; (2) diagnosis of the problem and consideration of alternative courses of action; (3) formulation of a strategy and of day-to-day tactics; (4) carrying out of the plan of action; (5) review, evaluation and stabilization of the change.[4] Theirs is a well-developed analytical approach which provides a concise framework for planning and action.

In this chapter and the following, we will turn to a comparable problem-solving approach adapted from several sources. This approach consists of four elements common to all similar approaches: assessment, planning, implementation and evaluation.

PROBLEM-SOLVING MODEL

Assessment: The Meat of the Matter

Assessing Interest The guiding rule for the assessment phase of planned change is "Do your homework!" Effective strategies for change must be grounded on a thorough and accurate assessment of the extent and nature of the *interest* in change, the nature and depth of *motivation* for change, and the *environment* within which the proposed change will occur.

The first question for a change-minded individual is a simple one: "Is anyone dissatisfied with the present situation?" If not, the situation does not lend itself to planned, directed, intentional change. We can look at it in terms of the "field force theory" developed by Lewin: at any given moment the behavior of an individual or of an institution is subject to forces which promote change and forces which resist change. No change will occur if the forces are in balance or equilibrium. For example, a nurse might want to complain to a superior about a serious problem in the unit that needs correcting; that is a force promoting change. On the other hand, she may fear that the superior will take offense and retaliate; that is a force resisting change. The nurse will not change her behavior—that is, actually go to the superior—unless the need to correct the problem weighs more heavily on her mind than the fear of possible retaliation. Assessment can be viewed as the task of identifying the forces that promote change and the forces that resist it and comparing their relative strength.

During this stage, the client or the people within the client system must be encouraged to admit any dissatisfactions they feel with the existing situation. It has to be understood that it is "all right" to concede an interest in changing things. Not only must the client or client system consciously feel the desire for change; even more important, the client must accept a share of the responsibility for initiating change. The client who says "By God, it does need to change!" can, in the next breath, suggest a lack of willingness to participate by adding, "The ANA should be working on that!" The person who seriously feels the need for change is asking, at the very minimum, "Is there something I can do to help it happen?"

Assessing Motivation By "motivation" we are talking about a process of stimulating people to act to accomplish desired goals. We are primarily interested in the motivations for job-related or professional behavior. Two of the leading theorists in this area are Maslow and Herzberg.

According to Maslow's widely cited theory, a person's internal motivation derives from what he calls the hierarchy of needs. He identifies our basic needs, in order from "lowest" to "highest," as physiologic, safety and security, love and belonging, self-esteem and self-actualization. We are motivated to satisfy the lowest needs first, then turn to the higher. Because modern society satisfies lower-order needs fairly well, Maslow feels that the higher-order needs have become the principal motivating forces in people's occupational or professional lives.[5]

Herzberg's theory revolves around two sets of factors which he describes as intrinsic or "motivators" and extrinsic or "hygienes." The intrinsic factors include such things as achievement, recognition, the work itself, self-growth, interpersonal relationships; these, he says, are the forces which determine job satisfaction. The extrinsic factors include such things as company policy, administration and supervision, work conditions and salary; these, he related to job dissatisfaction.[6] A study by Lamberton in 1970, based on the Herzberg approach, produced evidence that for hospital staff nurses the intrinsic factors of achievement, interpersonal relationships and recognition were in fact the primary motivating forces.[7]

More recent research has focused on the motivational factors which result from discrepancy between what an individual does, wants or expects and what he gets. This also can be described as the difference between what he sees as ideal and what he knows is real. In nursing we have an obvious example from the results of our survey, the difference between the level of responsibility nurses carry and the recognition and pay they receive, contrasted with other professions and occupations. Knowing how we feel about this, it is easy to see why the researchers have found that the self-identified discrepancy is one of the most powerful motivators of people. Also, the greater the discrepancy between real and ideal, the greater is the discontent and the more favorable the climate for change. A change agent assessing motivation must identify the nature and strength of these motivating forces in any client system. He has to find out: Is there enough motivation in the group to carry it through the process of change? If not, what incentives can be brought to bear to increase the motivation?

Assessing Environment The individual or group that is serious about change needs to recognize the importance of a favorable climate, or "environment," for creativity and innovation. Schaller and Libaw have identified twelve characteristics which indicate creativity and openness to change in an organization. In a broader sense, the same principles could be analyzed for any setting in which change is desired. The presence of the characteristics suggests that change is possible; their absence suggests areas in which work might be done to improve the climate for change. The twelve characteristics are as follows:[8,9]

1. The primary orientation of the organization or institution is to the contemporary social scene, rather than to the past, to pure tradition, or to perpetuation of the organization or institution itself. What philosophy pervades your agency, your school, your city's or state's "health care establishment?" Do its words and actions look backward? Do they seem better calculated to maintain the power of the in-group than to ad-

vance health care, education or nursing? Sometimes the philosophy will be visible in the style of dress, or in the relationships among the people—are they hierarchical or formal, or are they collegial and oriented to getting the job done?

2. There is an awareness that problems exist.
3. Throughout the organization or institution the primary focus is on people and people's needs.
4. The emphasis is on problem solving.
5. Persons within the organization are alert to the importance, relevance and availability of knowledge from a variety of disciplines that can be used by the organization in fulfilling its goals. Can you see signs in your setting that disciplines are recognized for their contributions, or are they seen as extensions of a main discipline?
6. There is continuing effort within the organization to monitor the pace of change.
7. The organization has a built-in self-evaluation mechanism to test its operations against its goals. Even in so nebulous an institution as the local "health care establishment" such a mechanism can exist; one might look, for example, to see if the planning mechanisms established under federal laws— most recently the Health Systems Agencies set up under the National Health Planning and Resources Development Act— carry real weight or operate as a rubber stamp for status quo thinking. A sign of a vital local health care system would be an HSA which carried out meaningful evaluations and had them accepted by the community.
8. There is widespread recognition and acceptance of the periodic need to change.
9. The financial administration of the organization focuses primarily on expenditures and output.
10. The leadership works hard to maximize the organization's problem-solving ability.
11. When new ideas are proposed, leaders know the points in the organization where intervention will be potentially the most fruitful.
12. To some extent, everyone in the organization is a generalist, and emphasis is placed on group processes and an open communication system.

It is worth noting that if individuals are totally committed to the organization or institution, the climate for change is weakened; it is also weakened if individuals within it feel alienated. If we follow the reasoning of Maslow and Herzberg, an ideal relationship between organizational and personal goals would seem to be one in which the individual sees the organization as an avenue for personal or professional growth. The primary rewards should be satisfaction derived from the change process, from professional growth and from the esteem of knowledgeable peers. The best climate for change appears to be one in which the problems are challenging but people feel personally secure.

The change agent who has carefully assessed interest, motivation, and the environment now has a working list of the factors which would promote the changes he seeks and those which would not. He can now identify ways to strengthen the favorable factors and minimize the unfavorable. Those strategies form the basis for an effective plan of change.

Planning: The Heart of the Matter

Support Group   Some of the earliest actions of the change agent are steps taken to broaden the base of support for the change, or to form a support group. The nature of the desired support group or power base will vary according to the nature of the client system and the arena within which the change is being pursued; obviously we would need a different support group for accomplishing changes within a health care facility than we would for seeking legislation to change a nurse practice act. In general, however, the support group brings a number of assets:

1. Numbers, which are important both for increasing the capacity for work toward change and for increasing the group's influence on decision makers. Numbers are especially important if the arena is a public or legislative one.
2. Skills which are needed to accomplish the group's tasks. A strong support group should include people with communications skills, even if the critical communications are one-to-one. If attractive, articulate, sensitive people are not chosen as spokesmen, the target group may well react to the person and fail to hear his message. People who know and can deal with the power centers important to the desired change—whether they are social groups, administrative structures or legislative bodies—also can be useful in the support group.
3. Credibility or status, which can be brought to a support group in the form of wealth, power, special knowledge, age, family name or individual, professional or civic stature.
4. Financial support, where this is important.

5. Contacts or connections with power, money, the mass communications media and so on.

A strong and loyal support group can broaden its power base by entering into coalition arrangements with other groups interested in the same specific ends. Coalition building, however, carries a possibility of greater need for compromise. Coalition building often comes later in the process, as part of strategy or tactics in pursuing goals.

Goals   As the support group comes together, it begins the process of formulating short-term and long-term goals and objectives and of considering strategies for and methods of evaluating progress. In this activity the process itself is critical; if it is an open and flexible process, it will draw on the interests and knowledge of all members of the support group. Not only will this make for better planning, but it will also draw the participants into a deeper commitment to the success of the effort.

The nature of the goals also is important. A group needs long-term goals as its target, and short-term goals as its mileposts. The goals should be realistic, appropriate to the change that is being sought, achievable within a specified time frame, and measureable. A firm, attainable schedule for achieving goals, established at the outset, is the best assurance that change will proceed according to plan; it also offers a series of yardsticks by which the group can measure how well it is progressing on the items that are important to the plan, not the peripheral items that inevitably present themselves for attention along the way.

A well-defined plan for specific action, periodically checked for results, also provides a built-in mechanism by which the group can reassess the realism of its strategy and, where indicated, change course. The fact that it is a clear plan makes it easier for changes to be decided by the same type of consensus as the original plan. The actual overall time frame for the plan will depend on many factors. The most important ones will be the complexity of the change desired, the number of people involved and the amount of education or communication needed for the change to be worked out.

In an effective plan for change, the goals must dictate the strategy. A successful strategy must consider the sources of power, and how that power is exercised within and around the client system. It must anticipate the types of conflict or resistance that will arise and provide means for coping with them. And it must include alternatives should the first course of action fail at any point along the way.

Sources of Power   It is not always a simple matter to identify the sources of power that will affect a group's ability to accomplish planned change. Power in our society is often diffuse and decision making difficult to pinpoint. People who wield power often can be identified, however, by their reputation, their visible influence on decision making, their ability to prevent issues from being aired, or their ability to deflect impending conflict. Their power may be derived from a vast number of sources—wealth, coercion, organizational connections, charisma, loyalties, understanding of people, technical knowledge, family name, age, tenure in office, organizational skill, ability to deal in rewards and punishments and control over the flow of vital information.

Besides identifying who wields the power, it is crucial to understand the way in which the power is used. Some styles of wielding power are subtle—for example, by deliberately withholding critical bits of information, a powerful individual can create discontent and dissension that lead to a desired result. By contrast, a powerful individual can operate by deliberately preventing conflict from coming to the surface. Sometimes power is exercised by deftly letting each potential dissident perceive that individual retaliation will be swift and devastating if he steps out of line. Whatever the strengths and style of the power users, the change-minded individual or group must take the time to understand how that power is maintained and used before acting. The plan lacking this analysis is a plan for futility, not change.

Often individuals at the head of an organization are believed to have power to effect change when in fact they have very little. Unfortunately, a bureaucratic structure will change only when its direction, values, orientation, and power relationships change; new leaders will be powerless to make significant changes unless they are able to influence these basic features of the structure. Each of the last several presidents of the United States has learned this truth, to his chagrin, after assuming office. Needless to say, in a complex bureaucracy or organization, power may be distributed in several centers, and often it is possible to accomplish changes by aligning with one or more of these existing power centers.

After analyzing the sources and use of power, the change agent or group should turn to analysis of the areas of potential conflict and resistance to the desired change.

Resistance to Change   Any attempt at change will be met with structural, cultural or psychological barriers, or resistances. Some of these will be placed in the way deliberately, others inadvertently.

Of these, the structural barriers are the easiest with which to deal. For example, consider a group which wishes to change a traditional, medical-model nursing school curriculum to an integrated, conceptually based curriculum. The group would quickly encounter the structural barriers—finances, the need for new clinical settings, equipment. While these might seem like major obstacles at the beginning, determination and a well-developed plan can secure money, clinical facilities and equipment. On the other hand, the resistances built into faculty attitudes and beliefs—the "human element"—may challenge the most resourceful change agent. Resistances from the people most directly involved and potentially threatened by change can be both subtle and formidable. These resistances require careful and imaginative handling by the change agent or group.

To analyze resistance, we must begin with an estimate of how the intended change will specifically affect the target system and the individuals within it. The next step is to analyze how the individuals are likely to react, based on their abilities, personalities and life experiences. The change agent can expect the greatest resistance from the groups or individuals who feel emotionally or intellectually insecure, who have invested a lot of their self-esteem in the status quo, who believe that the intended change clashes with their philosophies or value systems, who see it as a threat to comfortable social relationships, and/or who see no personal benefit from the proposed change. The person who works for planned changes must identify these people and make careful plans for reducing or otherwise dealing with their potential resistances.

At this stage there are several important things to keep in mind. First, any change of human behavior, or the perceptions, attitudes and values underlying that behavior, takes time. Any plan for change must allot enough time for the human impacts to be assimilated. Related to that is the fact that multiple, simultaneous changes will be more difficult to assimilate than step-by-step changes; given the natural human tendency for stability, change is easier to accept if important parts of the environment are held constant.

The practical-minded change agent will incorporate these factors into his thinking. For example, a nursing administrator who simultaneously tries to change the charting system on her unit from traditional to POMR, the type of nursing care from functional to primary, and certain clinical procedures, will likely meet massive resistance. However, if the administrator focuses first on the change in the method of charting and waits until this is successfully accomplished before initiating another change, she will have an easier time of it.

As another general rule, the methods and leadership style involved in a change effort can minimize resistances. If people in the client system do not like the change agent, that dislike will affect their thinking about the change as well; both perceptions depend on preexisting relationships between the system and the change agent. Resistance to change also generally will be less if the people affected by the change are involved in the planning for it and if their ideas are met with sensitivity and receptivity *before* the final shape of the change is frozen. By giving people who are potential sources of resistance a personal investment in the change, this strategy increases the prospects for its long-term success.

Sometimes change will involve a new role for an individual, or will require that individual to respond in a new manner to familiar situations. This could create resistance based on the individual's perceived threat to his self-image. If a veteran nurse needs to learn a new approach to a technique she has been performing for years, she may see the requirement as a slap at her professional qualifications; after all, she has years of experience. While such responses will vary from person to person, it is important that they be anticipated and that the individual's professional self-esteem be protected.

Resistance may show itself in many different ways, both overtly and covertly, ranging from hostility to complete withdrawal. The change agent must anticipate such responses and be prepared for them. For example, a change from traditional functional nursing to a primary care pattern may cause a veteran nurse to feel insecure and threatened; this may lead her to withdraw into a passive, nonparticipatory role. The veteran may not feel as insecure, however, if the change agent shares information with her and actually enlists her help in planning for and securing the intended benefits of change. This strategy can bring a register into the support group for change.

Deeper resistance may result from an individual's ego-involvement with the status quo. Change in this case may become as significant psychologically as the death of a part of the self. This is especially true if the "status quo" today is an innovation for which the individual had to fight sometime in the past; the reformers of yesteryear often are among the most vigorous resisters of change today. The change agent must be armed both with a clear knowledge of the benefits to be gained from the change and with a deep sensitivity to the values and thinking of the resisting individual or group. His strategy must be to show how the proposed change will enhance values or personal goals held dear by the resister. For change to proceed smoothly, this groundwork must be laid ahead of time.

Among conflicts that can arise in carrying out a plan of change, none are likely to be more crippling than those which arise within the support group itself. For example, the group may agree on certain needed changes but disagree on the means to achieve them; or conflict may center on the selection of allies, leadership styles, philosophical positions, definitions of purpose and personality idiosyncrasies. To prevent the group from polarizing around such issues, Schaller offers the following guides:

1. The group should work hard to keep open its internal channels of communication.
2. Dissent must be depersonalized. The ground rule is that members of the group are allowed and even encouraged to address the issue, but not to attack other members.
3. Each member needs to try to "look inside" the other's frame of reference, to understand his point of view.
4. The door must be left open for creative and meaningful participation by every member of the group.
5. Members of the group must have new opportunities to invest themselves in the goals.
6. The group should seek agreement on specific short-term goals.
7. Diversity must be recognized and accepted.
8. A sense of mutual trust must be cultivated.
9. Grievance mechanisms need to be established.
10. Events that have a paralyzing effect—real roadblocks—need to be recognized and dealt with.[10]

Beckhard suggests the "confrontation meeting" as a tool for dealing with conflicts within the group.[11] At such a meeting no hidden agendas are allowed; all views and feelings on the areas of tension are to be aired. The confrontation is followed by information gathering and sharing, the establishment of new priorities and timetables for action, review and evaluation. This type of open dealing with conflict promises several advantages:

1. It clarifies problems and procedures.
2. It fosters task-orientation and task structures.
3. It guides leaders to areas needing attention.
4. It quickly generates highly open communication.

5. It creates dialogue among different levels or segments of the support group.
6. It involves the group's members in "ownership" of the problem, and thereby increases all members' sense of responsibility for resolving it.

Developing Strategies Having studied sources of potential resistance and conflict and having identified possible means for coping with them, the group now turns to the development of a specific strategy. Here the first choice to be made is one of style of approach. The traditional style of seeking change has been through educational or persuasive means, or by some form of coercion, usually legal or legislative. These techniques work relatively slowly, and do not produce the quick successes that help to cement the loyalty and lift the morale of the support group. This may account for the recent popularity of the so-called dramatic witness approach to change, in the form of public demonstrations or other devices to grab the public spotlight and call attention to a problem or a need for change. One of the most adept practitioners of all time was Margaret Sanger. She perfected the art of getting maximum public attention with the least effort. Her acceptance of a jail term for disobeying what she believed was an unjust law anticipated the civil disobedience tactic of American civil rights workers by decades, and it was done with a flair that increased its public impact. Often a change-oriented group or individual will begin the process by using the dramatic witness technique and then, having established its visibility and solidified the support group, will turn to a more traditional, systematic approach of alliance building and "working within the system," just as Sanger did.

According to Schaller there are four general approaches from which a change-minded group can choose—coercion, co-optation, conflict and cooperation.[12] Coercion simply means applying authority or power to force a change; the group which selects this approach must concentrate its energies on gaining power. Co-optation means bringing the opponent into the supporting group, usually by promising something in return. This approach opens the group to more diverse points of view, but in some cases weakens the moral force of the cause by being perceived as "buying off" the enemy. An approach based on conflict or confrontation as its principal technique may serve to clarify issues, but often has a divisive effect even within the support group and stimulates resistances that may actually impede change.

The most widely used approach to planned change is the cooperative one. It requires skill in communications and interpersonal relations and can be very time-consuming, but it also can effectively produce change that will endure.

As the strategy is being selected, it is important that each member establish a meaningful identity within the support group. For many, this will occur as they are called upon to use their special skills. Group leaders should ensure that all members express their views and concerns, and that all are perceiving the plan in the same way; many a strategy has failed in implementation because a significant part of the support group suddenly realized that it had not understood the plan. There also should be an effort to develop a group identity, one which will give the group cohesion and reduce factionalism but which will permit expression of individual differences.

At the core of a change strategy is a clear, solid legitimate argument for the change based on logic and hard facts. Nothing will destroy credibility more quickly than a discovery that the cause for which one labors is based on incomplete or false data. Well-conducted nursing research is the best guarantee that this will not happen. Moreover, the arguments for the change must address the issues that are important for accomplishing the change; many a group has spent its energy developing eloquent arguments around issues that did not really matter to the success of its cause.

The argument must be presented in language appropriate to the target group. It should include proposals which will tend to build trust between the change group and the target; most often this can be done by emphasizing the issues that will be seen as most important by the target group. The argument is enhanced if it anticipates and deals concretely with likely consequences of the proposed change. For example, if you were discussing a proposal for a change to primary nursing with a group of nursing supervisors who were most concerned with status and authority you would emphasize the personal consequences to them in terms of status and authority. The argument must allow room for compromise within the long-range goals, and it must be developed in keeping with political realities. A state nurses' association may introduce a proposed new Nurse Practice Act which appeals to the most idealistic and aggressive among its members, and these members may organize an impressive march on the state capitol to show their support. Yet the proposal will falter if it does not incorporate the concerns of the less militant members who are in the majority, and if it allows no room for compromise. The more silent group almost inevitably will become just cohesive enough to let the legislature know that it has a larger following which is not quite so enthusiastic about the proposal. A group finding itself in this type of situation must be prepared to switch to an alternative strategy, which, if they have planned carefully, would have been developed at the same time as the original strategy.

If the change strategy involves redirecting the goals and values of an organization, the change group at some point will need the knowledge, approval and participation of the top echelon. Even so, such change takes time—by most estimates, two to four years for major organizational change. People throughout the entire organization must be acquainted with the proposed change and must see its relationship to the organization's goals. During the period of change, high priority should be given to increased communications within the organization, to better intergroup relations, to the satisfaction of needs of the members, and to a concerted effort to focus on *goals* rather than roles, on collaboration rather than competition, on *ideas* rather than personalities. Changes may not proceed at an even pace; they may begin, then lose momentum or cease. Often this happens because new people come into the organization and it changes. It may occur also because the group has focused so strongly on short-term goals that these have ceased to be means to an end and have become ends in themselves.

Crisis can be an important precipitating force for change— whether the crisis is real or only perceived. A perceived crisis heightens the level of discontent with the status quo, increases the attractiveness of new goals and makes it easier to generate discussion. The crisis presented by the deplorable conditions of British soldiers in the Crimea was an important precipitating factor in the development of modern nursing.

Legislation—or for that matter any rules which mandate behavior and which can be enforced—may either accelerate or retard change. Legislation can change behavior, and studies show that people's attitudes change along with their behavior so as to keep the two consistent. This is the psychological factor which allows coercive changes to endure. It is called cognitive dissonance, and it says that a person forced to behave in ways inconsistent with his beliefs will tend to resolve the conflict in the only way open to him, by changing his beliefs. In theory (though not necessarily in practice) a head nurse could apply the same principle in directing change by fiat; probably the staff would eventually see at least some merit in the task it was forced to do anyway. Examples abound in the consumer world. One of the most dramatic was the change in people's attitudes toward small cars after the oil shortage of 1974 and subsequent fuel price increases forced big cars out of many people's financial reach. Suddenly smallness was a virtue and "gas-guzzling" cars became a mark of vulgarity to people who previously took pride in the size of their cars.

Implementation: A Matter of Act

With its assessment and planning completed, the change group is ready to embark on the implementation of change—to transform its intentions into actual change behavior.

Throughout this phase, open communication is critical at all levels and in all directions. Everyone involved in the change, or affected in any major way, should know what is happening and why. Those who are working to accomplish the change need to know their exact roles, including the specific actions expected of them. To ensure that communication is kept flowing and that actions or problems are followed up, someone needs to work on implementing the change on a daily basis.

It it wise to "pilot" a proposed change on a small scale before implementing it broadly. The pilot effort should be carried out in a place where allies of the planned changes have been identified. For example, by changing nursing care first on a unit with strong leaders committed to innovation for better patient care, chances of failure are minimized. Once the change has been demonstrated successfully, and its advantages communicated its wider implementation becomes easier.

To sustain the motivation for change, it is important to establish recognition and reward systems for the people whose actions are furthering the change. These reinforcements can be verbal or nonverbal, and they can take the form of personal recognition, reassurance or support, economic or social reward. The important thing is to keep the individual worker aware that his efforts are visible and valued.

Evaluation: Does It Matter?

It is important throughout the action phase of the change process to follow through on scheduled evaluation steps—to pause at planned intervals and examine the progress against preestablished goals. Milestones successfully passed provide motivational support for the group, which can see the progress, measure the distance yet to be traveled and face its remaining tasks with growing confidence. Milestones which may not be achieved provide a basis for reexamining the realism of the strategy and for charting a new one where appropriate. It is important that the evaluation follow closely on the milestone if these purposes are to be served.

These are the key questions for evaluation:
1. Was the expected outcome realized? If not, why not?
2. Did any unexpected outcomes develop?
3. What areas need further planning efforts?

Stabilization

Once the point has been reached from which no further significant advance is possible or desired, it is time to stabilize the change. Various mechanisms may be used to accomplish this, including legislation, administrative action, or simply the group's commitment to the change. The stabilization is complete when the change has been internalized by those affected, and when it sustains itself autonomously. This stabilization is an essential part of the change process; it ensures enduring acceptance of change and prevents the client system from backsliding.

The goals have been achieved. If the process has worked at its best, the changed system is open, adaptive, restorative and permeable. Power is balanced and interdependent; respectful awareness exists among members of the changed system. They make decisions by consensus—they consider salient items, utilize valid and credible data, and face differences openly. The changed system is in "dynamic equilibrium." The change is stabilized. However, there is always room for innovation and improvement.

Here then is the process. Check your own understanding and ability to apply it in the situations which follow.

References

1. Marlene Kramer, *Reality Shock.* Saint Louis: The C.V. Mosby Company, 1974.
2. Thomas R. Bennett, *The Leader and the Process of Change.* New York: Association Press, 1962, pp. 45–55.
3. Alvin Pitcher, "Two Cities—Two Churches." *The Chicago Theological Seminary Register* (May 1967): 4–5.
4. Harvey Seifert and Howard Clinebell, *Personal Growth and Social Change.* Philadelphia: Westminster Press, 1969, pp. 83–93.
5. Abraham H. Maslow, *Motivation and Personality.* New York: Harper & Row, 1970.

6. F. Herzberg, *Work and the Nature of Man.* Cleveland: World Books, 1969.
7. Martha Lamberton, "Investigation of the Validity of Herzberg's Motivation—Hygiene Theory for Hospital Staff Nurses." Master's Thesis, University of Pennsylvania, 1970.
8. Lyle E. Schaller, *The Change Agent.* New York: Abingdon Press, 1972, p. 58.
9. Frieda B. Libaw, "And Now the Creative Corporation." *Innovation* (March 1971): 2–13.
10. Schaller, *The Change Agent,* p. 169.
11. Richard Beckhard, "The Confrontation Meeting." In Warren Bennis, et al., eds., *The Planning of Change,* ed. 2. New York: Holt, Rinehart and Winston, 1969.
12. Schaller, *The Change Agent,* p. 129.

FOUR

Doing It

Like Nightingale, Sanger, Wald and others, we have all encountered situations in our everyday practice that we would like to change. The situations developed and analyzed in this chapter are ones which have been identified as problems by nurses in response to the authors' survey. Some of the situations presented have actually occurred, others are simulated. Each situation has presented a challenge to the nurses involved and was resolved by them with varying degrees of success. Two situations are presented at the end of the chapter which have not been resolved. These are offered as challenges upon which you can test your own skills as an agent of change.

DAVID AND GOLIATH

"Oh, that makes me so angry," muttered Sharon as she wheeled the Teller newborn to the nursery.

"What's the matter?" asked Linda.

"Mrs. Teller wanted to nurse her newborn while she was on the delivery table or at least in the recovery room, and she isn't allowed!"

"Why?" asked Linda.

"Oh, Dr. Booker, the head of neonatology says the babies get too cold, and when they get to the nurseries they have trouble stabilizing their temperatures. I think it's a lot of crock! I can't see how the mothers' own body temperature wouldn't keep them warm."

Two days later Linda, a BSN graduate, approached Sharon, a diploma graduate working on her BSN, and said that she had been thinking about what Sharon said and agreed with her. She also said that in her nursing program the faculty always stressed that, if you identified a problem in your clinical practice, you should research it so you have a data base for proposing any policy changes. After thinking for a moment, Sharon saw Linda's point and agreed with her.

"Where do we start?" she asked, and told Linda that, while she used others' research in her nursing education, she was not taught how to carry out research herself. Linda said that she had not carried out a project in her program either, but had been taught the process and also had had to critique the research of others. Linda offered to get her notes and text on research that she had used. Both now became excited about the idea of setting up their own project to prove their point and to help consumers of their care get the services they wanted. They decided to meet for a few hours after work the following week.

At their next meeting Linda brought her notes and text from class. After a brief discussion they decided that their first step would be a literature search to see what other studies might already have been published in this area. They also discussed how they would introduce their idea to the head nurse and supervisor of the unit. Sharon was not sure how the head nurse would react, since she perceived her as being skeptical of the family approach to childbearing. They decided to discuss their idea in confidence with several other staff members for suggested approaches before going to the head nurse. More excited than ever, they decided to give themselves three weeks to research the literature and meet again.

At the next meeting they combined their results and found that there was only one somewhat related study in this area, and none that really addressed their problem. The next step was to write up their proposal and to discuss it with some staff members. A few days later on the unit, Linda saw her former teacher with a group of students and told her of the project. After congratulating her, the faculty member offered her support and suggested that they seek funding for the project. Meanwhile Sharon had begun discussing the project with some staff members who had all known the head nurse and supervisor for a longer time than Sharon. They almost all agreed that, even if the head nurse was not in total agreement with the idea herself, she was very supportive of her staff and took pride in their growth. The staff members with whom Sharon discussed the idea were supportive.

After preparing their proposal, Linda and Sharon decided to have Linda's former teacher review it. She made several suggestions which Linda and Sharon incorporated into the draft. Sharon had recently attended a nursing research conference at another local university and was impressed with one faculty member who was a keynote speaker. This faculty member, Barb Jones, was in charge of the research component of that program. They decided to contact her and ask her for her help.

Several weeks later, after incorporating the suggestions of both faculty into their proposal, Linda and Sharon were ready to present it to the head nurse and the supervisor. They chose a time when both were together and the tone on the unit was relatively quiet. The head nurse and supervisor read the proposal, asked several questions, talked it over between them and told Linda and Sharon they supported their idea. They liked the idea of nurses making decisions concerning patient care based on nursing research. They also warned Linda and Sharon that Dr. Booker was a very strong and opinionated person who would support his ideas forcefully. They suggested that the next move would be to make an appointment with the director of nursing to share their proposal with her. Linda and Sharon decided to send a copy of the proposal to her with a note about their plan, then schedule a meeting with her for several days later.

During the meeting with the director, the two became elated. The director wanted the staff to do more research, but the majority of the proposals she received had been poorly designed and stood little chance of succeeding. This project she believed could succeed, and she supported it. She told the two she would circulate copies of the proposal to the hospital research review committee and Linda and Sharon could present it to the committee at its meeting one month away. They also told the director of their plans to seek outside funding. She discouraged this because she felt the project required little money.

One month later Linda and Sharon presented their proposal to the research review committee and, with some discussion, it passed. The only stipulation made was that the research was to be carried out only when staffing was adequate. Unexpectedly, Dr. Booker was rather mild in his resistance.

Unfortunately for Linda and Sharon, the labor and delivery unit was very short staffed for the next several months, so data collection was slow. During their data collection over the next year, they perceived some resistance from several of their peers, and what they felt was a lack of support of the project. Almost one year later, they succeeded in gathering the data on a total of 100 newborns. They again contacted Barb Jones. She helped them run their data through computer analysis, and suggested ways of presenting their results.

The results clearly showed no significant difference between the temperatures of newborns who were breast-fed immediately by their mothers and those who were kept warm in heated transports. When Dr. Booker heard this he attempted to refute the results by arguing that the researchers used the wrong type of thermometer and that only glass thermometers were truly accurate.

Linda and Sharon discussed the criticism with Barb Jones. She pointed out that, because they had an adequate sample size and had used the same type of thermometer on both groups, any inaccuracies, if they really did exist, would be evenly distributed in both groups, therefore canceling out that effect.

As we leave this situation, the policy is in the process of being changed, and even now mothers are able to breast-feed their infants after birth prior to their being sent to the nursery. Dr. Booker has even begun thinking of redesigning the recovery room so that parents and infants can spend the first postdelivery hour together. Linda and Sharon (fictitious names) are pursuing publication of the results of their study. They succeeded; now let us analyze why.

Analysis
Assessment Sharon and Linda established early that there was *interest* in their project among their superiors and among other staff. Their superiors' varying *motivations* for supporting the idea were strong. The organization in which they worked was sufficiently open to change. The philosophy of the institution has a heavy emphasis on patient care, with research and teaching receiving a secondary place. Their project was aimed at improving patient care and was therefore consistent with the philosophy of the institution. Within the organizational structure they were supported by both their immediate supervisors and by the director of nursing. Throughout the institution there were other examples of innovations in the delivery of nursing care. Overall, it was an *environment* open to innovation.

Planning Early in the development of their project, Linda and

Sharon discussed it with other staff members and solicited their support. This was essential for implementation because other staff members would be involved in the data gathering. Their *support group* grew as they won approval of the head nurse, supervisor and director of nursing. They also had the support of two faculty members, Barb Jones being the key to the success of much of their work. The support group, as we analyze it, consisted of numbers of people (staff collect data); additional skills (the faculty connection); and power (head nurse, supervisor and director of nursing service).

The *goal* of changing the policy by carrying out the research was clear and easy for all of the group involved to identify and support. Not only that, it had meaning for each member. For Linda and Sharon it provided an avenue for personal and professional growth and a chance to see how they could actively effect change in their everyday practice. For the head nurse and supervisor it represented a chance to support growth of the staff and for nurses on the unit to participate more actively in policy issues. For the director of nursing service, two important goals were personal growth in her staff and the development of nursing research within the institution. The project supported both.

Linda and Sharon had identified and obtained the approval of *power sources* in nursing within the institution. The support of these people would be necessary in combating resistances from other power sources, most notably Dr. Booker, although others on the research review committee could also have presented resistance. The resistance the two felt from the nursing staff occurs commonly, possibly because the data collection is seen as an inconvenience, or because of inadequate time or possibly some envy. The project did not require new skills or new roles for the staff, so resistance from these areas was minimal. There was also little ego involvement in existing policy; had there been such involvement, it would have raised resistance. Fortunately the overall staff resistance was not great and the data collection was completed. Fortunately also for the group, there were not many other changes occurring at the same time. Since both Linda and Sharon were well-accepted members of the staff, they were acceptable *change agents*.

Linda and Sharon's strategy of educating the powers that be through the results of research was a method that had meaning for physicians, who base their practice on the results of scientific research. The method Linda and Sharon chose was one with which the target group was familiar and was presented in a manner they would readily understand. The method also placed these nurses on a collegial level in addressing this issue. It is very difficult to dispute well-conducted research findings without carrying out another study of your own or locating research findings of others which show contrary results. When Linda and Sharon presented their findings they had a strong case for changing the policy based on the desires of some parents and the logic and hard facts of their own research.

Implementation and Stabilization A new policy will be implemented, including the changes they desired. But both Linda and Sharon plan to keep a close eye on the temperature of the newborns who are breast-fed immediately to prevent a breakdown in technique that might lower newborn temperatures and scuttle their efforts.

We all have to congratulate these two nurses. Here is a prime example of two staff nurses starting with no particular power base, pulling together and capitalizing on each other's skills. They worked within the system and implemented the change which resulted in improved nursing care and underlined the talents of nurses in the eyes of physicians. We also must congratulate the staff, head nurse, supervisor and director of nursing service for creating the environment and lending the support that allowed it to happen. What was your latest David and Goliath situation?

STRAIGHT TO THE TOP. . . . AND BACK!

Three staff nurses who worked on a medical-surgical unit of a large urban teaching hospital met in the coffee shop to discuss the obstacles they were encountering in attempting to deliver comprehensive care to their patients.

Jean, a verbal, assertive registered nurse, felt that the 50-bed unit demanded at least four professional and two nonprofessional personnel to adequately staff each shift. Her colleagues, Susan and Donna, wholeheartedly agreed. They could not understand why Mrs. Fleck, the head nurse, believed that optimal care could be given with only two RNs and two aides for the evening and night shifts.

As Donna saw it, Mrs. Fleck wanted the majority of her staff working the day shift, Monday through Friday. This, she felt was because Mrs. Fleck herself always worked days, never worked weekends, and never involved herself in direct client care. Donna saw Mrs. Fleck's attitude and approach to both staff and patients as purely administrative. "She wants to please the hospital administrator by keeping her budget well-controlled; that's why she locks the supply closet."

Susan related a recent experience with Mrs. Fleck. "I approached her about the quality of care we were able to give during the evening shift. Her response was, 'We'll discuss this at our next unit meeting.' Believe me, she's not receptive to changes in the staffing situation. I think she believes that we are the problem; we're too idealistic."

The three decided to explore this problem with other RNs and auxiliary personnel on the unit. Jean planned to meet with each worker. She established her timetable so that all professional and auxiliary personnel would be contacted within a two-week period for their opinions and suggestions. The three also decided that Mrs. Fleck should not be included in these discussions because they saw her as extremely rigid, satisfied with the status quo, and always resistant to any changes in the institution. Donna felt that the head nurse would demonstrate her resistance by exploiting the individuals seeking change by scheduling them for all evenings, nights, holidays and weekends. The trio felt their best strategy was to organize the RNs, LPNs, and aides, and write their concerns in the form of a petition. This would be presented to Mrs. Wills, the nursing service administrator, whose philosophy, expressed at the most recent inservice meeting, was to "deliver holistic, professional care to patients."

Proceeding with her plan, Jean contacted all professional and auxiliary personnel on the medical-surgical unit. Although she did not find that all the 27 workers were convinced that the situation was desperate, she did succeed in organizing a support group. Jean encountered resistance from four recently graduated RNs who did not agree with the strategy. They told Jean that they believed that staffing did inhibit the quality of care delivered, but they felt that Mrs. Fleck was receptive to staff needs and concerns and should be contacted before a petition was sent to the nursing service administrator.

Jean felt that the four could "minimally" block her efforts. However, she did not anticipate the support that these young nurses generated. One of the new nurses who liked Mrs. Fleck developed a counterstrategy; she informally contacted all the workers on the unit and pointed out the dangers of working in a covert coalition.

The end result of both strategies was a polarization of the workers on the unit. Jean's group continued to push for change. They developed the petition signed by 15 of the 27 staff members and submitted it to Mrs. Wills, the nursing service administrator. It read:

"The majority of personnel functioning on this medical-surgical unit petition you to explore the staffing patterns of the unit. We believe that our situation demands immediate attention and that our patients' welfare is jeopardized."

The four new nurses generated a great deal of support for Mrs. Fleck from the remaining 12 workers. They also contacted the nursing service administrator—lauding the efforts of the head nurse. Feeling loyalty toward Mrs. Fleck, they also informed her of the efforts of the other group.

The nursing administrator handled the petition by organizing an open forum discussion for the personnel on the medical-surgical unit. She did not invite the head nurse to this meeting. After exploring both groups' impressions of the situations, the administrator shared her feelings with the group. "I do not approve of your tactics; I suggest that you present this problem to Mrs. Fleck. She has the ultimate power and authority to administer her own unit and resolve this situation. You must take your concerns to her."

Analysis

Assessment Once they had established their own common interest and desire for change, Jean, Donna, and Susan determined that there was considerable *interest* among other staff members for seeking increased staffing, as well as some *motivation*. Not all of the latter, however, was related to the quality of patient care. The interest and motivation were assessed in terms of the strategy (increased staffing) rather than the basic goal (improved care).

The trio failed to assess adequately whether the hospital *environment* was conducive to change. They did perceive the nursing director's philosophy as being supportive of comprehensive care and, thus, likely to be supportive of the change. They failed to look for evidence throughout the institution that might have validated this assumption, or that other problems in the organization were acknowledged and addressed. They also failed to find out what other changes had been previously attempted on the unit, how they had been handled, and how long ago these had occurred. They failed to validate their perceptions of the head nurse's ideas of the staffing situation and quality of patient care being delivered on the unit. They themselves had in no way documented a lack of care on the unit, or shown that by increasing the numbers of staff the situation would improve. In short, they had done little of their homework.

Planning The trio did see a need for and did establish a sizeable *support group*. Their original *goal* of improving patient care was often sidetracked by the group members' personal needs to be relieved of some of their workload. The lack of a clear focus on the goal prevented them from establishing a plan with short- and long-term goals which would have included documentation of a lack of care on the unit and a projection of the benefits from increased staffing. A rational plan like this would have at least been one that the administrative staff could evaluate.

In their planning, the group identified the head nurse as a source of power. They failed to recognize that, since her power was delegated within a hierarchical structure, Mrs. Fleck would be supported by her superiors unless they could clearly document that she had abused her power. They also failed to analyze other possible power sources that might provide assistance or resistance. They totally underestimated the resistance to their strategy that emerged from within the staff; nor had they even thought about how they would deal with it. Because of their lack of assessment and planning, energies of both groups were soon focused on an intergroup struggle which resulted in tension and polarization on the unit. Focus on the goal of improving patient care, a goal upon which staff and administration could agree, was lost. Any attempt to effect change with as little assessment and planning as this group did is calculated to get the group straight to the top and back—quickly!

PAPERWORK TO PEOPLEWORK

Mrs. Miller is the new head nurse of a 40-bed medical unit staffed by 11 professional nurses and seven auxiliary personnel. She recently became aware of discontent among the professionals, who feel they are overburdened with nonprofessional activities. Some of the staff say that this has been a significant factor in a recent high staff turnover rate on the unit.

From listening to the staff concerns, Mrs. Miller gathers that the professionals would like to spend more time giving direct patient care and that they would also like to further their own professional development. She believes that the staff discontent might be reduced if she could hire a unit clerk to relieve the nurses of clerical activity, and could begin a staff development program.

Before requesting additional staff, she realizes, she must first document the need. She develops a form to survey the workload of the professional staff. It focuses especially on the time spent both in nonprofessional activities and in direct patient care. In a second section of the form she seeks to learn whether the nurses want more direct patient care, whether they are interested in a staff development program and what kinds of staff development activities they see as needed.

The survey shows that the average amount of professional staff time spent in nonprofessional duties is about four hours per shift. Eleven of the 14 staff members are interested in participating in a staff development program, and all 14 are interested in more direct patient contact.

Mrs. Miller decides to informally survey the patients' perceptions of the amount of time nurses spend with them. She finds that the overwhelming majority of the 60 patients with whom she talks wish that the nurses could spend more time with them, although they realize that the staff is very busy with other things. Some of the patients are not as understanding nor as tactful when asked. It is clear to Mrs. Miller that more direct patient care is needed.

She presents the findings of the staff and patient surveys to the director of nursing services and requests a unit clerk for the floor. Mrs. Miller also is armed with data from the nursing literature which document the benefits of having a clerk on the unit.

The director, Mrs. Wells, is impressed by the homework Mrs. Miller has done. She also is a little concerned about the results of the surveys. While she is not totally convinced that a unit clerk is the answer to the concerns being raised, she is willing to provide an additional staff person for a six-month trial period. At the end of that time Mrs. Miller is to demonstrate how that individual has made a difference in the cost or quality of care. Mrs. Wells also approves the idea of a staff development program but is interested in learning what kinds of outside resources the staff feel are needed to support such an effort.

Mrs. Miller now holds a meeting of the unit's professional staff. She tells of her meeting with the director and of the temporary hiring of a unit clerk. She also discusses what she feels the new staff member will be doing. As she views it, he would order supplies, complete the patient charge slips, schedule diagnostic tests, stock the closets and note physicians' orders. He would work from 9 A.M. to 5:30 P.M., Monday through Friday. Since the physicians make rounds between 8 A.M. and 9 A.M. and again from 4 P.M. to 5 P.M., the clerk would note the majority of physicians' orders. He would also ensure that all shifts had adequate supplies. When she finished, Mrs. Miller asks the staff for further suggestions, and incorporates these into the plan. She makes it clear to the group that the position is temporary unless it can be documented that the clerk's presence makes a difference.

Mrs. Miller also discusses the results of the second part of the questionnaire, which show a unanimous desire for more direct patient contact and a nearly unanimous desire for a staff development program. The questionnaire has shown that individual members of the professional staff have differing needs in their own professional development. Mrs. Miller asks how the group feels about having each member establish her own personal goals for development for the next six months. As part of this plan, each staff member would address how she was going to increase her direct patient contact. Mrs. Miller also wants each member to identify what outside resources or support she needs to help her reach her professional development goals. At the end of the six months the staff would evaluate their success in meeting their goals and would set new goals. All members of the staff like the plan.

Following this meeting Mrs. Miller also schedules individual interviews with nonprofessional staff members so that she can allay any anxieties they might have. She explains that the changes are designed to promote better care for patients and allow more room for staff to develop their abilities. She encourages each nonprofessional staff person to discuss her own personal job-related goals, and provides counseling and support for all of them on an individual basis. Thus, while the nonprofessionals are not part of the general staff discussion, Mrs. Miller is able to draw them into the program by giving each of them an individual stake in it.

During the next six months, Mrs. Miller documents all problems in patient charges for supplies, scheduling of diagnostic tests, missed physician orders, and staff complaints about nonprofessional demands on their time. Near the end of the six months it is clear that problems in each of these areas have decreased as compared with the previous six-month period. It is also clear that professional staff morale has improved. As a result of the staff development program, three of the professionals are developing nursing research projects which will benefit the entire unit.

Mrs. Miller repeats the first part of the survey of six months earlier and finds that her professional staff members now are spending an average of 2.5 hours per shift on nonprofessional activities. She begins another informal survey of the patients and finds such a marked difference in response that she asks the nursing director to accompany her while she talks with the remaining patients. It is apparent to both of them that patient satisfaction has increased over the preceding six months. The combination of the patients' responses, the documented decrease in professional time spent in nonprofessional activities, increased staff morale and the decrease in problems of scheduling, tests, patient charges and missed orders are enough to convince the director. The ward clerk is now a permanent member of staff.

In conferences with staff members it is evident that each member has enjoyed setting her own goals for professional development and has liked measuring progress against such goals. The nurses also feel that the head nurse had been very supportive of their goals. At the end of the staff conference, Mrs. Miller compiles a list of outside supportive resources that can be used to enhance the staff development program. Having achieved her first goal, Mrs. Miller is currently working to bring more of these outside resources to the staff development program. She has also begun to make long-range plans for a transition to an all-RN unit.

Analysis

Assessment *Interest* and *motivation* for change are evidenced in this situation by the level of discontent among the staff nurses. The desire for more patient contact is shown both on the staff survey and patient survey. Later Mrs. Miller increases the staff's motivation for increased patient contact by asking staff members to incorporate this into their personal goals for professional development.

Mrs. Miller, upon being hired, had known that the hospital's management philosophy was consistent with progress, and she was able to find evidence of innovations in patient care in several units in the hospital. She also established that the director of nursing was supportive of reasonable, planned change.

The staff on the unit has had to adjust to changes periodically, but since Mrs. Miller's arrival 12 months ago little has been occurring. Mrs. Miller's assessment of the *environment* leads her to believe it will support change efforts.

Planning In planning for the change, Mrs. Miller seeks *support* from the staff by informing them of the survey results, the efforts she is making to change the situation, and the results of her meeting with the director. Mrs. Miller also seeks and obtains the support of the director.

The *goal* of the unit is to increase patient and staff satisfaction by increasing the amount of professional time spent in direct patient care and by initiating a staff development program. The goal has been discussed at length with the staff in the context of the staff's own concerns and desires expressed in the staff survey and of the patients' documented desires. The goal is a clear one supported by the staff and director as well as Mrs. Miller. Her plan to hire a unit clerk is clearly related to the goal and understood by the staff and director.

Mrs. Miller identifies the director of nursing as the *power source* holding the key to her ability to hire the clerk and work toward the goal. She knows that a well-reasoned and well-documented problem and action plan are the best way to overcome *resistances* the director might raise to investing in a new unit clerk. She knows that Mrs. Wells is concerned with both patient and staff satisfaction and will be supportive of a good plan for dealing with any documented problem in these areas. Mrs. Miller minimizes any possible staff resistances by involving the staff directly in the definition of the problem, and the planning and identification of the goals. Resistance also is minimized because the staff directly benefits from the change. Potential resistances from the nonprofessional staff members are minimized by Mrs. Miller's added personal attention to them.

Implementation and Stabilization   Upon receiving approval of the director, Mrs. Miller promptly *implements* the plan, involving the total staff. She gives the nurses a stake in the plan's success by stressing the temporary nature of the new clerk position and the need to show benefits if it is to be made permanent. Responsibility is clearly defined for each part of the plan, and the documentation of problems is a continuous evaluation tool. The thorough evaluation of the project's success results in the director's approval of the permanent staff position, stabilizing the first part of the change. The staff development program is stabilized by the setting of personal goals for the next six-month or twelve-month period, and by Mrs. Miller's planning for supplementing the basic program with outside resources and support. The key to stabilization, however, is the overwhelming staff support for the program after its first six months.

We must congratulate Mrs. Miller for being an exceptionally thorough planner and sensitive administrator of her unit. We must also commend the director for her willingness to invest in improved quality of care on the unit without demanding an immediate reduction of other expenses to offset the cost of the new clerk. (It seems likely that Mrs. Miller's direction of change ultimately will produce more cost-effective care.) And we must commend the professional staff for its highly professional response to the head nurse's initiative.

IDA HAMMER—BUT DIDN'T USE IT

"I wonder what new project Ida has cooked up for us this month," said Pat Hill, Assistant Director of Nursing Service, to her colleague, Jenny Miller, Coordinator for Staff Development. Both were on their way to the monthly nursing administration meeting.

"What makes you think we're about to be faced with a new project?" Jenny asked.

"Well, all the telltale signs are present," replied Pat. "After Ida returned from that evaluation conference two weeks ago, she's been making rounds on all the floors and talking to a number of head nurses and staff. Last week, she asked me to get her copies of the job descriptions for the various levels of nurses, and a sampling of staff evaluations. She took the material, and some articles from the library and locked herself in her office for the next few days. When she finally emerged, she was smiling. And if that isn't enough to convince you, did you see what she is wearing today? Her Halston copy. That's the outfit she always wears when we're about to receive one of her 'earth-shattering' ideas."

"It's those ideas that frighten me," said Jenny. "I'm just beginning to recover from the sessions I've been holding with the staff on primary nursing. Many of them were just beginning to feel comfortable with team nursing, and now its on to primary nursing. Actually, I guessed something was up. Just a few days ago, Ida was asking me how the inservice team identified programs for staff development. She was also interested in knowing whether we used the performance appraisals of staff nurses to help identify what programs were needed. I told her that the comments on most of the evaluations were so general that it would be difficult to identify staff development needs from them. I also added that we had our hands full trying to keep up with our present programs without trying to plan and implement new ones."

Pat and Jenny were the last two members of the administrative staff to arrive at the meeting. Celia Sun, an assistant director, six clinical supervisors and Ida Hammer, Director of Nursing, had been waiting for them.

Ida had been Director of Nursing at this 250-bed acute care facility for a year and a half. For the year previous to her new appointment, she had been an assistant director of nursing in charge of inservice programs at a large metropolitan hospital. While she had many years of clinical and a small amount of administrative experience, Ida left her last position because she saw it as an essentially "dead-end" job. She had decided that the only way to set many of her ideas into motion was to assume the leadership role at this relatively newer, smaller facility. Prior to accepting this position, Ida had spent a good deal of time talking to the hospital administrator, director of medical services, and the members of the nursing administration. She felt that the philosophy of the institution was progressive, the director of medical services was generally supportive of the autonomy of nurses, and, as long as she finished the fiscal year within her budget, the hospital administrator was willing to give Ida free rein in running the nursing department.

During her first year as director, Ida had maintained a rather low profile. She realized after she accepted the position that some conflict had surrounded her appointment. Pat Hill, who had been Assistant Director of Nursing for seven years at the hospital, and who had many important contacts and friends within the institution, had also applied for this position. Ida soon realized that Pat had some feelings of resentment at being "passed over" for the job of director, probably because she lacked a master's degree. The fact that Ida was much younger and had less administrative experience than Pat only added to Pat's feelings. She also became aware that Pat commanded a good deal of respect among the nursing staff, especially with many of the older nurses. So Ida bided her time and spent most of the first year getting to know her staff and trying to become accepted by them as well as assessing the needs for change.

When she began her second year as director, Ida started to set into motion many of the ideas she believed would benefit the patients, her staff and the institution. She was very anxious to become recognized as a leader. Ida carefully planned all of her ideas before presenting her proposals to her administrative staff who would be responsible for their implementation. Normally, before finalizing a proposal and presenting it to the staff, she took time to speak with all members of the group, individually, seeking their input and assessing who was supportive and who was resistant. She attempted to have proposals reflect a synthesis of these individuals' ideas. She found that this approach led to better acceptance of her ideas.

While this approach had generally been satisfactory, Ida was very concerned about the amount of time it took to set her ideas into motion. She also began to realize that Pat Hill and Jenny Miller could be counted on to offer criticism of her suggestions at group meetings, even though these were not voiced at the individual meetings she held with them.

Jenny had been hired about the same time as Ida. She had just obtained her Master's Degree in Nursing and was functioning as a clinical specialist. Ida soon found that Jenny had little knowledge or experience in administration and that she had some insecurities in assuming her present role. Pat Hill had taken Jenny under her wing when she started in order to "show her the ropes." The resulting alliance had caused Ida some problems in building group support for her goals.

In her current project to initiate peer review as a mechanism of quality assurance, Ida had decided to try to circumvent the resistance offered by Pat and Jenny. She had been reviewing with Celia Sun, her other assistant director, the existing mechanisms for evaluating nursing care. Currently there were basically two. Staff nurses did self-evaluations of their nursing care and also were evaluated by their superiors. Ida believed that a more effective evaluation system could be achieved by adding peer review.

In addition to Celia, Ida had shared her ideas and sought input from three of her six clinical supervisors. These three individuals had been most supportive of her ideas in the past. She decided against meeting with the other three clinical supervisors since two closely aligned themselves with Pat and Jenny and the other had very little to offer at any time.

Ida felt that the time was ripe to initiate the current project. Annual self-evaluations and administrative evaluations for merit and promotion had just taken place. She believed that the project therefore would not be seen as a mechanism to document inadequacies. Some of the staff members who had just completed their first self-evaluations had told Ida that they had found it to be a very profitable experience but added that they often wondered how their own perceptions of their care compared with those of their patients and colleagues. Many had also expressed a desire for a planned program to help them work on their areas of weakness. Some of the staff nurses felt that evaluations by their superiors were very limited and sometimes inaccurate since these individuals were not able to observe them on a day-to-day basis. When questioned by Ida, most said they would be very interested in having their nursing care evaluated by peers.

At today's meeting, Ida was ready to present her proposal calling for the initiation of peer review as a mechanism for quality assurance. The project was to be initiated on two units, 3B and 5A. These units had been most receptive to change in the past. The proposal called for a three-stage program to be completed three months hence. The first stage of the proposal was a consciousness-raising experience in which the staff and administrators from the selected units were to participate. The consciousness-raising experience was to develop the group's understanding of what peer review involved and to have members verbalize their concerns about a process in which individuals evaluate the results of each other's performance. The second stage of the proposal was to have outside consultants work with the two groups in identifying the criteria for evaluating peer performance. The third stage involved the actual evaluation.

Results were to be shared with staff members being evaluated and with the director of nursing. Ida would analyze the data to assist the inservice staff in identifying staff development needs. The needs would then be addressed in programs developed by this department, coordinated by Jenny Miller. The two assistant directors, Pat Hill and Celia Sun, were to work closely with Jenny on program development.

Since Ida realized that the whole concept of peer review was often perceived as a threat, Ida had Celia Sun, an individual respected by the total administrative group, initiate discussion of the proposal with the group. After the proposal was read and discussed, Ida called for a motion to accept the project. Celia made a motion and it was seconded by one of the supervisors who had been previously informed of the project. Discussion concerning the proposal was limited and Ida noted with interest, that neither Pat nor Jenny had anything to say. When the vote was called, the motion passed. Of the nine voting members, five voted yes and there were four abstentions, Pat and Jenny among them.

When the meeting was over, Pat and Jenny decided to go to dinner together. Over cocktails, both noted that while they had not been previously informed about the project, it was evident others were. Pat questioned the hidden agenda behind their not being informed. Jenny wondered whether peer review was to be used for documenting inadequacies without their realizing it, or if Ida felt Jenny currently was not meeting inservice needs of staff. During dinner, Pat and Jenny discussed further possible meanings the proposal might have. They decided that it was time to show Miss Hammer their own power within the institution. By the time they had finished dessert, Pat confidently remarked "I can't wait to see this new idea backfire. Ida may have won this battle, but she's not going to win the war." Indeed, three months hence Pat and Jenny had aroused enough suspicion and resistance to the project on the two units that the group failed to complete phase two. Let us analyze why.

Analysis

Assessment   Ida began with a fundamental error. She failed to assess the *interest* and *motivation* for change in terms of the long-range goal, improving the quality of patient care. This error was especially glaring since clearly her interest grew out of her recently reinforced awareness of the pressure for quality assurance in nursing services. Ida's assessment of staff interest did not even touch on this possible source of interest and motivation. Rather, it focused directly on one mechanism she had chosen to work toward in accomplishing the goal, peer review. Possibly Ida fell into a common trap for insecure administrators—a fear that open discussion might result in a challenge to her choice of both goal and means.

Even within the narrow focus of her assessment, it was, at best, a perfunctory appraisal. Informal discussion with a few staff nurses was hardly adequate to judge interest in a potentially threatening change. Moreover, of the nine members of her administrative staff—the people who would have to make the system work—she only consulted four. By focusing defensively on her power struggle with Pat Hill, she failed to really analyze the problem at hand.

Her assessment of *environment* was more thorough. She had determined before coming to the hospital that it had a progressive philosophy and was supportive of nursing. She had thoughtfully decided to pilot the peer review on two units where staff had previously proved receptive to innovation. Generally, she had correctly assessed the environment as conducive to successful planned change.

Planning   During the planning stage Ida did very little to increase her *support group*. While Ida herself was clear on the long-term *goal* of change, improving the quality of patient care via improved nursing care, it was not a goal made clear to others. Attention was focused instead on the short-range goals of establishing a peer review system and of adapting inservice programs to the needs identified through this system. These goals, too, were essentially Ida's. While they had been discussed with a minority of the members of her administrative staff, there had been little participation by the staff in their actual choice. In fact, four of the nine members of the group had chosen to withhold their support of the goals in Ida's ill-advised "vote" on them. (Ida was lucky. She went to a vote being sure of only four votes. Had all five of the others gone to the other side, she would have boxed herself into an instant failure.) The time frame selected for instituting peer review was too short, given the complexity of the goal, the lack of involvement of the administrative staff in its planning, and the group's obvious divergence on it.

Ida clearly failed to analyze the *power sources* which would bear on the success of the project. While she utilized the power of one of her assistants, Celia Sun, she neither analyzed the power of Pat Hill nor took steps to enlist it or neutralize it. The most important power base on which she failed to capitalize was her own. Ida, in fact, seems to have a great deal of trouble handling power, whether it is her own or others'. On her arrival as a new administrator, she would have had adequate power to either win Pat's allegiance or isolate Pat on the nursing staff; instead, she had "bided her time" for a year, working to "win" acceptance and shrinking from the use of rewards or sanctions to establish her authority. Even now, Ida could probably have split up the Pat-Jenny alliance by making Jenny (along with Celia) a third corner of the key planning group. In a sense, she surrendered Jenny to Pat before the battle began. Moreover, had she been a little more shrewd and self-confident, Ida would have been looking for some way to draw Pat and her undeniable power into the support group. While Ida's frustration is understandable, no change agent at any level of authority can afford to simply ignore a major power source in her planning.

Ida's decision to exclude not only Pat and Jenny, but three of the clinical supervisors from the advance discussions increased the *resistance* to the plan. Ida had anticipated resistance on the target units and had arranged to deal with this through the "consciousness-raising" exercises. While she had expected the excluded administrative staff to be upset at her tactics, Ida did not look far enough ahead to spot the very real risk that these individuals would actively encourage the resistance of the unit staffs. Ida's failure to discuss the plan with Jenny, whose role as service coordinator would put her in the middle of the planned change, was a gross error, strengthening Jenny's impulse to align herself with Pat. Resistance also was stimulated by the timing of the proposal. Staff throughout the hospital, still adjusting to changes from team nursing to primary care, reacted negatively as rumors of the new change spread quickly.

Finally, while Ida had the positional power to effect the proposed change, she failed to use it. Additionally, she was not totally accepted as a *change agent* among a significant portion of the total staff. Had she worked to convince Pat of the need for change and given Pat the role of change agent, resistance would have been greatly reduced.

In summary, there was insufficient interest and motivation for the change, at least as it was presented to the staff. The goal lacked clarity and general acceptance. The time for implementation was too short. The strategy ignored significant power sources and failed to anticipate and deal adequately with the resistance. Ida had a hammer, but she certainly didn't use it!

BACK TO THE DRAWING BOARD

A few faculty members within a college of nursing were discussing some concerns raised at an instructional staff meeting. A number of faculty members had expressed interest in increasing and refining their clinical skills. Many were also concerned about the quality of some of the clinical experiences students were having. This second matter was a problem that was resurfacing with increasing frequency. The number of nursing education programs in the area had increased dramatically over the last ten years; schools were competing for use of the available facilities and, as a result, quality clinical experiences were difficult to find. Hospital and other agencies were beginning to exert more and more control over student experiences in their efforts to assure quality patient care.

As four of the faculty members discussed the problem, Amy, an individual with a wealth of both practice and teaching experience, had a brainstorm. "Since most of us are looking for opportunities to improve our clinical skills and all of us want better clinical learning experiences for the students, let's consider how one solution might answer two big problems," she said. "What if we were to establish our own clinical agency? We could call it Nursing Unlimited."

The group laughed and jokingly started to add dimensions to "Nursing Unlimited."

"Sure, we'd all hang up our shingles."

"Yes, and we'd get incorporated."

"I'll bet there would be a real run on the market when we showed up on Wall Street."

Sharon, who always had her feet on the ground, helped to bring the group back to reality.

"Do you know how many blood pressures at 25 cents a piece we'd have to take in order to rent a building?"

"And where do you propose we get all the equipment?"

"Are any of you cited in Howard Hughes' will?"

The group eventually moved on to other topics. But Amy was not to be stopped. She decided that Nursing Unlimited was a viable concept, if funding could be generated through a grant proposal. During the next ten days, Amy canvassed five key faculty members seeking potential support in the coordination of such a project. She selected the five on the basis of their strengths in understanding community structure and resources as well as their administrative capabilities. Of the five, three were very interested in pursuing this project; one said she would be interested in the implementation phase; one commented that she would need to see what kind of administrative support the university would give before committing what she thought would be a considerable amount of time.

Amy spent the next four weeks surveying the literature for any precedent in which faculty had established an agency run entirely by nurses. She found a few such precedents, but very little information about the process of setting up such a facility. To get this information, she next consulted a few of the individuals responsible for starting this type of agency. She found three of these individuals willing to serve as consultants in the development of the project proposal.

Amy now felt she was ready to meet with the Dean of the College of Nursing to share the idea of Nursing Unlimited and to present an outline of her project proposal. She was anxious to learn how much support she might anticipate from the Dean.

Amy's meeting with the Dean left her with more questions than answers. On the whole, the Dean, an individual with years of administrative experience, supported the project proposal. She did, however, voice three major concerns: How did Amy plan to obtain the needed community support for such an agency—lay and professional? Since grants fund for a limited time only, what other sources of funding were available to ensure that the agency would become self-sustaining? More specifically, what would be the relationship between this agency and the college? The Dean obviously was not anxious to have to assume an additional financial burden. Finally, what were the legal implications for nursing faculty and students in an independent practice?

Amy now realized that a project of this magnitude required nursepower! She saw four possible options:

1. To decrease the nature and scope of the project, making Nursing Unlimited a long-term goal.
2. To develop a project proposal committee of approximately six faculty members, with two members working on each of the major concerns raised by the Dean. All members would collectively develop the grant proposal.
3. To work in collaboration with the existing nursing services in the defined community to establish this agency.
4. To scrap the entire project.

To assist her in deciding, Amy called together the three faculty members who had expressed interest in Nursing Unlimited. After about five hours of discussion and many cups of coffee, this small group made the following decisions.

1. Nursing Unlimited would become Nursing Limited. The scope of this practice would be limited to the following:
   a. Physical assessment of elderly adults in a community of need.
   b. Group teaching sessions with elderly, focusing on unique health needs of this population.
   c. Referral to appropriate health agencies of individuals with problems not within the scope of this practice.
2. A grant proposal committee would be formed.
3. A group of individuals representing nursing and working with elderly in the community of need would be asked to meet with the proposal committee to collaborate in planning and implementing the project.
4. The project would roll!!

The proposal committee involved Amy, the three members who had originally offered to participate and two other faculty members chosen by this group—one because of her knowledge of the needs of the elderly, the second because of her physical assessment skills.

The committee worked for two months to define the nature of the services that would be provided and to identify the community of need. Three consultants were approached to assist the committee with the planning. The group had selected three possible target areas for Nursing Limited. Using statistics from the county planning commission, the committee was able to document a dramatic increase in the elderly population in one of these target areas. Projections showed that this trend was expected to continue for the next ten years.

One committee member familiar with community resources encouraged the group to focus on this particular geographical area. She felt that the services Nursing Limited expected to provide would be needed within the community. An ad hoc group was established to contact all the area hospitals and a few of the outpatient facilities serving the defined community. The group's report indicated that the services of Nursing Limited were needed in the target area. The group became very excited over this piece of information and asked the ad hoc committee to write a report listing the places contacted, responses to their requests for data and to place this information on file for future reference.

At this juncture, the committee decided to meet with representatives from the various nursing services within the community to discuss plans for Nursing Limited. Clare, a member of the committee, was asked to contact the directors of these services. Clare had just recently graduated from her master's program where she had focused on the needs of the elderly. Prior to that, she had worked for two years in a hospital setting.

Nurses representing the Community Nursing Service (CNS), neighborhood health centers (NHC), nursing homes and rehabilitation centers were asked to participate in the meeting. After hearing about the project on the phone, all directors eventually agreed to send representatives. The individuals contacted at the nursing home and the rehabilitation center responded very positively to Clare's phone presentation. The nurses from the CNS and NHC seemed less enthusiastic; in fact, the nurse from the NHC asked to see a copy of the proposal before she agreed to send a representative to the meeting. Perceiving a negative feeling in this nurse's response, Clare decided to address it openly to validate her impression and to determine if she could address the nurse's concern. The NHC nurse's response was: "From the sounds of it, we already are performing the services you described. I believe that such a facility would result in duplication of services. But I'm willing to read your proposal before I make a decision."

As Clare got off the phone, she made a mental note to find out as much as she could about this nurse and the services provided by the NHC prior to their meeting. She also wanted to find out more about the other facilities, their services and the type of nursing administration in each agency. She realized that support from agencies in the defined community was essential. The project consultants had informed the proposal committee that it was necessary to document such support in the grant proposal in order to expect funding.

The meeting with representatives from the nursing service agencies was set for the first week in February, just two weeks away. The proposal committee was anxious to meet a March 15 deadline for submission of the grant application. During those two weeks, the members of this committee were very busy meeting their individual teaching responsibilities. They were able to get together only once to prepare their presentation for the agency representatives. Clare neglected to share with the committee the response to her phone presentation from the representatives from the CNS and NHC. In addition, she decided to wait until after the upcoming meeting to find out about these agencies and the services they offered. The day of the meeting arrived. After the proposal had been presented, the director of nursing for the NHC asked to address the group. This director clearly delineated the services offered not only by her facility, but also by all other agencies represented. The context of her remarks clearly indicated that she had been in contact with all of the agencies' representatives and that she felt that Nursing Limited was a duplication of services already offered by the existing facilities. From her remarks, it became evident that this director believed such an agency would jeopardize continued use of and support for existing facilities. She suggested that the proposal committee seek another community where these services were lacking. Support for the proposal came from the representative from the nursing home, but this was weak at best. All other representatives agreed with the director of the NHC, despite the best efforts of the proposal committee to change their minds. After the meeting had ended, Amy and her committee met to discuss where they should go from here. It was obvious from their tone that it was back to the drawing board.

Analysis

Assessment   Her discussion of the problem of clinical facilities gave Amy a clear idea of the faculty's *interest* and *motivation* for a project such as Nursing Limited. The faculty members were interested in maintaining and enhancing their own clinical skills, and in assuring the quality of clinical experiences for their students. Within the college of nursing, the *environment* also could be viewed as favorable for change. The Dean was receptive to Amy's ideas, assuming that every measure was taken to ensure that Nursing Limited would not become a liability to the college. Had the proposed change affected only the faculty and the college, Amy's assessment of interest and motivation would have been on target.

However, the group failed to realize that it also was proposing to institute a change in the target community. While it did compile statistics to show an abstract need for the services to be provided by Nursing Limited, the group totally failed to assess the interest, motivation and environment for change in the community itself. It did obtain data from the planning commission, yet there is no evidence that the planning commission was sounded out as to whether it felt services were needed, and if so, what kind. All other contacts were with existing health care providers in the community. The committee failed to make sure it understood the services and philosophies of these agencies before it presented its plans to them. A thorough assessment would have required that members of the committee actually visit the agencies and learn about them firsthand, that it identify the agencies' own perceptions of problems in the community, and that it couch its proposal in terms of those perceptions. The most serious error, however, was in confusing the agencies with the community. A true assessment should have leaned heavily on consumers of service, ranging from the managers of union pension plans to associations of retired people, including militants like Gray Panthers. Perhaps the committee's consultant had neglected to mention that strong consumer endorsements would carry weight with granting agencies—and indeed might help win acceptance for such a project, however grudging, from the agencies, too.

Planning Within the college, Amy and, eventually, the committee, carefully built a *support group* for the change. Members of the group were chosen carefully for the skills they could bring to it. Almost no attention was paid, however, to the need for a support group in the community. The committee did not attempt to anticipate the *resistances* that might occur in the agencies, or to identify potential *power sources* in the larger community which might have been recruited into the support group. Partly because they tried to work within a time constraint that was too limiting, the committee made errors that increased the resistance. They failed to consult the community agencies until their plans were already well developed. Instead of going to the community to sell the idea patiently and calmly, they summoned the agencies to a meeting. The summoning was done, moreover, by an individual with relatively limited experience in effecting change.

In short, the committee's strategy simply did not take into account the need to involve the community, and especially consumers, in the earliest stages of planning for community services. It is of little wonder that this particular attempt at change did not get to the implementation phase. The assessment and planning for Nursing Limited at the community level was most certainly just that . . . very limited!

IMAGE: SAY WHAT YOU DO AND DO WHAT YOU SAY

Joanne D., a graduate nursing student, was invited by the public relations committee of the local district nurses' association to share the results of her master's thesis with the group. Her research was a public opinion survey on the image of nursing in Youngsville, a medium-sized industrial city. She told the committee she had interviewed a scientifically selected sample of the population and had found results which clashed with her own concept of professional nursing.

The survey showed that, in general, the people of Youngsville County saw nurses as helpers who acted only at the direction of physicians. They thought of nurses' education as vocational training after high school and did not think that nurses either desired or necessarily should have a voice in formulating health care policy. They did, however, view nurses as very caring individuals who were usually willing to answer questions and spend time with people. They also believed that nurses had the technical skills to comfort the sick and injured.

"This survey shows that we are favorably regarded by people in Youngsville," Joanne concluded, "but we are esteemed as people who care, not as professionals. I wanted to share this with you in hopes that you, as the PR committee, can do something to modernize the public image of nursing in our city."

Following the presentation, the chairperson, Cynthia S., a young associate director of nursing at Youngsville General, asked for discussion. Each member of the committee knew of incidents which reinforced Joanne's findings. Margaret J., a public health nurse, mentioned that her PTA group had canceled plans for a special program for parents on adolescent health problems because no physician had been available to speak on the scheduled nights. Although Margaret had offered to recruit a qualified nurse for the program, some members of the PTA argued that only a doctor could properly conduct such a program. Others felt that few parents would come if the speaker were a nurse.

Janet P., an educator active in affairs of the nurses' association, noted the district's frustration in trying to make itself heard by the Comprehensive Regional Health Planning Commission, which was now being changed under new federal law into a Health Systems Agency. The layman who chaired the outgoing planning body had deferred almost unquestioningly to physicians and hospital administrators and had treated nurses who appeared before the body with polite indifference.

Cynthia reported how a major new wing of Youngsville General had been designed and built with little consultation with nurses. As a result, the nursing service was being forced to live with a physical arrangement which, among other things, required extra nursing time for the distribution of medications. The committee agreed that it was time to modernize the image of nursing, but how?

Janet recalled that a fellow educator, Sally F., was married to a public relations professional with considerable knowledge of health care. The group decided she should be contacted. Cynthia called Sally and asked if she would serve on the committee. She also asked if Sally could recruit her husband, Richard, as a volunteer consultant for a project to improve the local image of nursing. Sally and Richard came to the next meeting of the committee. Richard said that he would be able to attend an occasional meeting and to make suggestions to the group, but that he had no time to do any work, such as writing PR materials or developing lists of contacts in the news media.

Richard asked a lot of questions, so many that at times the nurses on the committee began to feel irritated. He asked about the study, and a lot of questions about how nurses felt about their image. Did it make them feel angry? What specific things made them feel this way? Weren't some nurses content to be doctors' helpers and to leave all the decisions to the doctors? Did the poor image of nursing result in some concrete ways in poorer health care for the public?

Did it contribute to higher health care costs? How? If improving the image would require a lot of volunteer work by nurses (not just the committee), would many nurses be willing to do it? If the volunteer work would help solve community problems at the same time it improved nurses' image, would there be more willing volunteers? The committee agreed that it would be possible to show that nursing's image affected the quality and costs of health care adversely. The group was not entirely certain how large a proportion of local nurses were unhappy with their image or how much time they might wish to volunteer.

Richard asked the committee if it could identify a few critical health care problems in the community. After some discussion, the committee named three. The visiting nurse service was unable to keep pace with the increasing workload resulting from earlier discharge of patients from hospitals. The community lacked comprehensive aftercare services for former mental hospital patients. And there was a disturbing increased incidence of preventable childhood diseases, especially measles, among Youngsville children.

Richard noted that he had seen a tiny newspaper article about the measles problem, but had not even heard about the others. Was the public in general as uninformed as he about them? What were nurses doing about the problems? One committee member said that the district had been working quietly on the visiting nurse problem. The executive director of the community nursing service was retiring. The district nurses' association was trying, so far unsuccessfully, to persuade county officials to provide the service with new, larger offices and a more adequate administrative budget. Cynthia reported that nurses had made progress, although more limited, on the other problems as well.

"I think you have the basis for a successful program to create a more modern image for nursing," Richard told the committee. "But it will require the enthusiastic support of the district board and of a fairly large number of concerned nurses." He explained that the major part of a program to change the local image of nursing would be for nurses to assume active leadership in solving the community health problems. These activities would provide substance to back up a public relations campaign. It might take two years of intensive work to make much impact on the general public's perceptions, he said, but it should be possible to identify lesser goals for shorter time periods.

The committee members were enthusiastic. They understood

Richard's point that it would be easier to get nursing discussed in the news media if it were actively involved in community problems. They believed it would be possible to find nurses concerned enough to work on and speak out on the problems they had identified. Richard pointed out that nurses were already taking a leadership role in the community nursing service problem, but that they just had not made their role publicly visible.

The group decided that changing the public's image of the educational preparation of nurses, their relationship with physicians and the role of nurses in health policy would be long-term goals. The committee's short-range goals would be to establish highly visible leadership in the three identified areas of community need. At Richard's suggestion the committee also decided to try to establish nurses as a recognized source to which the news media would turn for information about health issues. The first task would be to sell these goals to the district board.

At the next district board meeting, Cynthia presented a report highlighting the findings of Joanne D.'s study. The PR committee requested authorization from the board to conduct a mail survey of the membership regarding its feelings about nursing's image. Cynthia explained that an effective campaign to improve nursing's image would require a fairly large volunteer effort by nurses. The survey would stimulate interest in such a project. She also mentioned the three areas of community health need in which the committee saw nurses' activities as a basis for an improved image of nursing. The board authorized the survey and scheduled discussion of a possible PR campaign approach as the principal agenda item for its monthly meeting two months later.

During the next week Cynthia contacted the two nurses who were heading the effort to strengthen community nursing services. She learned that the agency director's official retirement date was just ten weeks away. She also learned that the chief opponent of the new offices for community nursing services was the county commissioner in charge of finance. He approached the situation as part of a politically popular effort to "hold the line" on county taxes.

Recalling an article in the state nurses' association newsletter, Cynthia did a little research and discovered a similar situation in which nurses had shown that strengthened community nursing services could postpone the need for an addition to the county home for the aged. The leader of that effort, Eileen K., Ph.D., was now an officer in the state nurses' association. A little more research showed that a projection of trends in Youngsville would lead to considerable pressure for a new wing on the county home in less than two years.

Cynthia discussed the findings with Richard, then called the district president, Genevieve B. She told her that the district could probably generate publicity and momentum on the community nursing service issue with a well-planned dinner to honor the retiring director. Cynthia volunteered to chair a committee to organize a dinner as a special project of the PR committee, if the district could gamble about $100 for advance expenses which would probably be recovered. The dinner was approved, and Eileen K., Ph.D., was secured as the featured speaker.

Cynthia and Sally developed a survey questionnaire. It addressed nurses' reactions to Joanne D.'s findings, their concerns about various community health problems, and their willingness to volunteer for community work or PR assignments. Sent as part of a regular mailing to the district's 900 members, the survey drew 345 responses, an excellent 38 percent return rate.

A solid majority of the respondents felt that nurses were "put down" by people, and not taken seriously as professionals. About 120 said they would be willing to spend two hours per week on volunteer work, especially if it would solve community problems and improve nurses' image at the same time. However, almost none wanted to chair task forces or otherwise take organizing responsibility. Only a few expressed interest in public speaking or working as contacts with newsmen or public officials. The survey results confirmed that psychiatric aftercare, hospital discharge follow-up and childhood immunizations were community problems about which nurses were concerned.

Sally and Cynthia had been busy talking with friends and colleagues in psychiatric and pediatric nursing about the aftercare and immunization problems. They encouraged several concerned nurses to join together and share their concerns with the district board. They told the nurses that the district would be more receptive to the idea of assuming active leadership in these areas if the nurses volunteered to help. As a result of this encouragement, two groups of nurses approached the district president and asked for time at the next board meeting to discuss psychiatric aftercare and immunization. Following their presentations the board authorized two special task forces "to work with other community organizations and the PR committee" to find solutions to the problems of psychiatric aftercare and the increasing incidence of preventable childhood diseases. Cynthia wrote an announcement of the formation of the new task forces and mailed copies to the news media.

The PR committee now concentrated its efforts three ways. Several committee members worked on plans for the recognition dinner. Sally and another member worked with Richard to organize a weekend workshop to develop PR skills for nurses. Cynthia prepared a report to the board on the PR committee's plan for improving the image of nursing.

At the next board meeting, Cynthia introduced Richard as a volunteer consultant. He explained to the board that effective public relations had to be organized around what the district was *doing*, and that it had to be related directly to the interests of the target audience (the general public). Joanne D.'s survey had shown high public recognition of nurses' dedication and ability to comfort patients, but low recognition of nurses' educational qualifications and ability to act independently and to exercise leadership in health care. The answer would be to emphasize these latter characteristics in any PR effort. This could be done by a slow, patient, one-on-one effort to persuade community leaders that nursing's role had changed. However, another approach could work faster.

"This could be accomplished," Richard continued, "if nurses assumed visible leadership on health care problems that were of major concern to the general public." The PR committee had already informed him that the district was pushing for solutions to critical problems in psychiatric aftercare, childhood diseases and community nursing services. These were issues that could be dramatized both in terms of emotions and health care costs. If the district wished to modernize the image of nurses in Youngsville, he would suggest that its strategy be to make its leadership in these three areas more visible.

Following Richard's comments Cynthia presented the PR committee's goals of establishing visible nursing leadership on the three community problems and of establishing nurses as a respected source of health care information for the media. Even though these were goals that could be pursued by the committee on its own, the board's endorsement was needed for two reasons. First, the program would require a great deal of volunteer activity and the board's endorsement would help in recruiting nurses to work.on it. Second, the costs for paper, mimeograph supplies, postage and stationery necessary for the project might amount to $250 above the committee's normal expenses.

The project itself called for training approximately 15 nurses in PR skills and a systematic program by which these nurses would develop contacts with the news media. In addition there would be intensive media work around the district's activities on the three major community problems, including a special promotion around the recognition dinner for the retiring director of community nursing services. The survey had demonstrated nurses' interest in the project and had produced volunteers.

Cynthia also asked the board to authorize the legislative committee chairman to make the legislative "hot line" available to the PR committee for occasional use in radio news promotion. (The hot line was a telephone number nurses could dial to receive recorded messages on new developments in legislation which affected nursing. It was sponsored by the legislative committee and shared with four neighboring districts as a regional project.) The legislative chairman reported that all the neighboring districts had agreed that the hot line could be used for PR activities if these could occasionally reflect their own local needs.

One board member argued that if there was going to be a major new PR effort it should be devoted to the state nurses' association's legislative priorities, especially a current battle over respective licensing requirements for RNs, LPNs and Physicians' Assistants. Cynthia replied that this was indeed important, but that it was of much less interest to the general public and could not serve to improve nurses' image as effectively. Richard suggested that the creation of a positive image of nursing leadership would strengthen nurses' influence on such legislative issues in the future. After some discussion, the board decided that it would give the long-range objective of improved image a higher priority at this juncture.

At a workshop two weekends later the PR committee and 12 other nurses were introduced to PR skills. Richard and Sally led. They explained that the first rule for getting good news coverage is to do something newsworthy. It is easier to get attention for your activities, however, if you also cultivate relationships with people in the media. You begin this by studying your newspaper, television and radio outlets.

One nurse was assigned to each of Youngsville's two daily newspapers, two TV stations and six radio stations; another to the four small weekly neighborhood newspapers. Each individual was assigned to follow the news and public service programs of his or her medium. All were to keep careful notes on who wrote or broadcast news or public information about health care, what was said and what attitudes it reflected. This would help in deciding how to approach the news people who wrote about health regularly. They were also told to research as much as they could about editors, managers and news specialists in their media outlets by using two reference works, *Editor and Publisher Yearbook* for newspapers, and *Broadcasting Yearbook* for TV and radio. Both of these books were available in the library, but Richard brought a copy of each to the workshop so the nurses could do their research on the spot.

One nurse noticed that the managing editor of the morning Youngsville *News* was the same man she had heard the medical director of Youngsville General talk about as a golf partner. Richard said that, because the managing editor was the ultimate decision maker on news, this information could be significant in two ways. First, it suggested that the managing editor was familiar with the medical viewpoint and probably would react negatively to news releases slanted antagonistically to physicians. Second, it meant that the medical director might be an especially influential ally if he could be recruited to publicly support a given cause, such as the strengthening of community nursing services.

Richard emphasized that to attract TV news coverage it was necessary to identify some visual interest. The news assignment editor would want to know what was happening, why it was important and what his crew could film to make it interesting to viewers. People talking would not usually be enough, unless they were celebrities. He cited as "sure winners" two recent TV news items. In one, the local lung association had held a press conference on air pollution on an open plaza overlooking the city's smokiest zone of small industries. The viewer could actually see pollution as it was being discussed. In another, Youngsville General had dramatized the opening of a new intensive care unit by holding a press conference in a circle of working monitors. The equipment was placed so that cameras filming the medical director and oscilloscope screen would also catch out-of-focus images of the unit staff hurrying back and forth in the background. Similarly, radio stations like to have voices of newsmakers on their news shows. Because they usually have small news staffs, it is often necessary to try to provide such quotes by telephone.

"When you talk with a newsman, be forthright," Richard said. "Give him straight answers. Admit it if you don't know something and offer to find out for him. Provide him with clear, concise background information. A one-page fact sheet is as much as most newsmen ever need. Above all, don't ever try to con a newsman. If he makes a mistake or misquotes or misrepresents you, by all means write a letter to the editor or news director. But phrase it as a correction of fact and don't attack."

Broadcasters, he noted, are required to devote broadcast time to public service as a condition of holding federal licenses. They do this in two ways—by broadcasting special programs as a public service, including call-in shows giving listeners an opportunity to state their views, and by airing special 10-, 30- and 60-second "spots" which are akin to commercials on public service topics. Any non-profit organization can suggest topics for public service programs dealing with community problems. They can also submit tape-recorded or videotaped "spots" with educational or charitable purposes (but not to further the organizations' pure self-interest). As part of their licensing requirements, stations must consult with community interest groups about community problems, document the groups' input and then show how their programming responded to the problems. Usually a group that expresses interest can become a part of this process. Cable TV franchises often make so-called public access broadcast time available at off-hours for community groups that wish to put on their own programs. The groups then publicize these on their own to attract viewers to them.

The workshop also covered speakers' bureau operations. The basis of a good bureau is a list of speakers who are knowledgeable about particular subjects. If possible two or more speakers should be available on the most important topics. The repertoire can include one or more "canned" slide talks, for which scripts or detailed outlines are provided and the speaker's role is to deliver the standard talk and handle questions. Speakers are publicized through newsletters of federated clubs, such as Lions, Rotary or women's clubs, and by leaflets or flyers mailed to other clubs or civic associations, posted on health facility bulletin boards or distributed at major public events. While advance publicity for speakers is usually up to the sponsoring group, the speaker's bureau can generate extra publicity by issuing news releases about the speeches being delivered by its members. These should be sent two to three days ahead of time so that they can be used in the media immediately after the talk has been delivered.

Nurses at the session had their first chance to apply their new knowledge in connection with the dinner recognizing Eleanor T., the retiring community nursing service administrator.

When the dinner was still four weeks away, enough tickets had been sold to Eleanor's friends to ensure that the dinner would not lose more than $50 or $60. One committee member then initiated publicity by sending news releases (short suggested articles) to the city editors of the newspapers and the news directors at the radio and television stations. This first release simply announced the dinner, who was being honored and why, and the guest speaker. This was to get the dinner mentioned in print and on the air to attract attention and reservations.

About a week later a slightly more elaborate release emphasizing Eleanor T.'s career and accomplishments was sent to the family (formerly women's) editors of the daily newspapers and to the local weekly newspaper serving Eleanor's neighborhood. This was to generate interest in a possible feature story on Eleanor T. and to make the family editors aware of the dinner. About ten days later releases were sent, again to the city editors and news directors, emphasizing the expertise of the guest speaker, Dr. Eileen K., in cutting health care costs. This was to attract more attention to the dinner, if possible, but also to alert the editors to the cost issue.

Meanwhile the group had carefully worked to be sure that the proper VIPs were invited, including the city's health commissioner, the county commissioners, the medical director of Youngsville General, presidents of the County Medical Society and specialty groups, the executive director of the Health Systems Agency, the local League for Nursing and editorial writers for the media. The state nurses' association president also was invited. Cynthia made special efforts to ensure that the county commissioner in charge of finance attended. She had invitations sent to the governor, both U.S. senators, the two congressmen whose districts included portions of greater Youngsville, and the regional director of the U.S. Department of Health, Education and Welfare. Knowing that most of them would not come, but realizing that officials often send messages on such occasions, she attached a brief summary of Eleanor T.'s accomplishments and the significance of community nursing services to their invitations. This was worded in such a way that it could be used almost word-for-word in a congratulatory telegram. One week before the dinner she called the officials' offices to ask if they were attending or sending messages. The governor, both senators, and one congressman sent telegrams. The other congressman sent his administrative assistant. The regional HEW director sent his ranking nursing administrator to represent him at the dinner.

Four days before the event Cynthia sent a "news and photo

memo" and a press kit to all the media. The memo simply outlined in half a page the event, the people involved, the time and location. It also gave explicit instructions on where news media people should come, who they should ask for information or assistance, when and where they could go for interviews, photographs or taping. The press kit included a program, a complimentary press ticket for the dinner, a general news release on the occasion, a picture and profile of Eleanor T., a picture and thumbnail biography of Eileen K. and a one-page fact sheet on how the speaker had reduced the need for costly nursing home beds by strengthening community nursing services. The fact sheet prominently mentioned that experts in Youngsville had predicted that a $1.5 million addition would soon be needed by the county home if something were not done to reduce the growing demand for beds there. The same theme was boldfaced in the news and photo memo itself. Apart from the time it took to prepare and the cost of the free dinner tickets, these kits cost about $2.00 each to assemble and mail. The committee had prepared one for each of the 14 media outlets, and several extras.

In the press kit sent to the radio stations, Cynthia also enclosed a note saying that for the 24 hours preceding the dinner, by calling the hot line number, the station could get a recorded 60-second statement about saving health care dollars. They would hear Dr. Eileen K., a nurse who had proved that community nursing services could lower health care costs. This statement was recorded soon after Eileen arrived for the meeting. It was then placed (with a brief introductory comment by Cynthia) on the tape machine activated by the hot line telephone number.

In preparing the press kit, Cynthia had spent some time talking with Eleanor T. She prompted Eleanor's recollection of bygone incidents in which community nursing services had enabled older people to remain in their homes long after it seemed as though they would have to move to nursing homes. Cynthia encouraged Eleanor to share those recollections with the guests at her dinner, since the principle of community nursing was, in fact, to help people stay well and at home.

Four reporters, two photographers and one TV film crew came to the dinner. Genevieve, the district president, as toastmistress, read the congratulatory telegrams. The guest of honor spoke warmly and movingly about community nurses helping people. The guest speaker spelled out a future for community nursing that clearly linked the human side to hardheaded considerations of cost-effectiveness. Cynthia noted the finance commissioner, who had been seated next to Dr. Eileen K. during the dinner, was taking it all in. Cynthia herself made sure that the HSA executive director, who was seated next to her, did not overlook the planning sophistication reflected in Eileen's presentation. Sally had seated herself with an editorial writer from the morning *News* and made certain that he understood the issue being raised and the background.

Following the dinner the PR committee met to review the coverage. It had worked out well. Both newspapers, morning and afternoon, carried accounts of the dinner, dividing emphasis between Eleanor T. and the cost issues raised by Eileen K. Both TV stations carried items—one a fairly well-developed item with film of the dinner. The other was a briefer mention showing the still pictures of Eleanor T. and Eileen K. Two of the radio stations carried Dr. Eileen K.'s quotes taped at the dinner. Three others used the quote from the hot line. On the second day the morning *News* carried an editorial strongly suggesting that the county commissioners review whether their position on community nursing services was the best long-range approach to saving tax dollars.

A further payoff resulted from a casual conversation one PR committee member had had with a reporter from the *News*. He had commented on Eileen being called "doctor." The committee member had remarked, "Oh, there are two nurses with doctorates working right here in Youngsville." This led to a Sunday feature story headlined "This Nurse Is a Doctor!" profiling one of the two and noting the increasing educational levels of nurses and their effect on health care.

Five weeks after the dinner, and following meetings with nurses, physicians, county administrative staffers and the HSA staff, the county commissioner of finance announced that he had concluded that expanded community nursing services would save tax dollars in the long run. He would support moving the program into larger offices and increasing its budget. Three reporters immediately called the district nurses' association for comment on the decision. Phase one had been a resounding success. The district was now ready to move on to phase two. It was also enjoying an influx of new and renewed memberships.

Analysis

Assessment In this complex situation, assessment occurred on several levels because change had to occur on several levels. On one level it was necessary to change the behavior of nurses in Youngs-ville. They had to become more actively involved with community problems in order to change their image. Thus the PR committee's first major assessment task was to test the *interest* and *motivation* of nurses to become more active. The interest was demonstrated not only by the answers to questions on the PR committee's question-naire, but by the exceptionally high rate of response. Motivation was evidenced by the number of nurses willing to make a specific commitment of two hours per week to work on community prob-lems.

The whole project actually tied into two different motivations—a desire for nurses to be respected as professionals and a professional concern over unmet health needs. It was also apparent that the *envi-ronment* within this district nurses' association was one of openness to change. This was evidenced by the board's receptivity to the PR committee's problem-solving approach, by the leadership's open communications channels (the hot line, the ready recruitment of board members to give dinner invitations to VIP acquaintances, and so on), and by the financial backing given to the PR committee.

At another level, Richard guided the committee into an assess-ment of the community's *interest* and *motivation* to change its per-ception of nurses. The PR consultant is, in effect, a change agent whose goal is to change perceptions, or levels of awareness, in a target group. His questions forced the PR committee to think beyond nurses' frustrations and analyze the possible interests of the consumer—the public—in the situation. The discussion focused on people's interest on quality health care they could afford. The as-sessment here actually was weak because the PR committee never took steps to validate that the public (as opposed to nurses) was concerned about the three problems. The nurses also made an as-sumption, not unreasonable, that the public would respond to pocketbook issues. While Richard referred to costs in his presenta-tion to the district board, there was no real effort to validate the as-sumption.

Normally an effective PR person would test such assumptions in conversation with news people. This would give him a feeling at least for the receptivity of the media to a given issue. A third level of assessment, in fact, would be of the media. The nurses wished the media to change the way they reported health issues so that nurses appeared in a more up-to-date light. The careful study of the news media growing out of the workshop was designed basically to

provide nurses with enough knowledge of the media to make judgments about media *interest* in various issues. Nurses also need to
judge potential media *motivation* by gauging how many people
might read, watch or listen to any particular subject. A nurse who
can say, "Almost every patient in our hospital asks about . . ." has
tapped a source of motivation for a news person to pay attention.
An observation about editors' golfing companions might provide a
clue to the media *environment* for specific kinds of reporting.

Planning The PR committee carefully built its *support group*. It
drew members from the nursing community at large by means of
the survey. The nurses most interested in the three major problems
were attracted by the idea of getting more PR and overall support
for their work. The legislative chairperson probably felt that by
providing the PR committee with access to the hot line she would
strengthen the support base for her pet project. This gave her a
stake in supporting the project. One of the shrewdest additions, of
course, was to bring Sally into the project, her husband's PR skills
in tow.

By focusing attention on the retiring Eleanor T., the group succeeded in creating an event which effectively linked altruistic nursing ideals to the image of modern professionalism it sought to foster. The *goals* were fairly clear, though not readily measurable. The
strategy for pursuing the first step was well developed, even elaborate. However, this was an ambitious project calling for a sophisticated strategy. In the workshop, the nurses clearly focused on the
major *power source* for changing public perceptions, the media.
They also worked hard to involve many community power sources
(political and health care leaders) in their activities, and dealt capa-
bly with two very key power sources (the county commissioner in
charge of finance and the executive director of the HSA) at the dinner. They even used the attention-getting power of Eileen K.'s doctoral degree to their advantage.

Implementation In the implementation of phase one, the nurses
used a certain amount of overkill. Had the dinner been *merely* a tes-
timonial to Eleanor T., the number of news releases would have
been wasteful. One release ahead of time and one at the time of the
dinner would have been sufficient. The higher powered approach
served the district's political goal of expanding community nursing
services.

If the PR committee is astute, it will pause briefly at the end of
phase one. It will make certain that the full support group shares

the excitement of this success, and it will reassess the situation for phase two. In dealing with a problem like immunization, and certainly more so for psychiatric aftercare, the nurses will find a more complex and often conflicting set of public reactions. These issues will be more controversial, and a more thorough assessment ahead of time will better prepare the nurses for these efforts.

CATCH 22

A group of 15 undergraduate junior students in an upper division nursing program get together one day in the student lounge and decide to do something about what they perceive as a lack of clinical experience in their nursing program. They decide first to develop a questionnaire and poll the entire junior class to see if the other 50 members, as well as the senior class, feel as they do. Kathy and Lisa, two good students with writing abilities, are asked to do this. Lea and Judy, also good students, are given the task of researching the literature to see if they can find studies that might back up their case. The group decides to meet in two weeks.

At the next meeting the group has increased to 47 students, 30 juniors and 17 seniors. Kathy and Lisa report that 85 percent of the junior class want more clinical experience while 70 percent of the seniors would support such a move. They have also compiled the reasons students felt more clinical experience was necessary. Lea and Judy have carefully researched the literature and have found eight studies they feel support their position. There is much discussion and a feeling of excitement in the group as Lea and Judy present each study to the group. After much more discussion, the group forms a plan. They plan first to meet with the faculty and present their feelings, results of the questionnaire and studies they have found that support their case. If they are not able to get satisfaction from the faculty, they plan to schedule a meeting with the dean. They also plan to have their position published in the university newspaper if they need more support, and to use some of the student strategies from the sixties if necessary. As the meeting breaks up, there is an air of excitement and cohesion among the 47, with a promise to bring their friends to the next meeting. Lisa and Kathy are to make arrangements to meet with the faculty.

The nursing faculty consists of eleven full-time teachers. According to a recent faculty workload survey, faculty members now spend an average of six hours teaching each week, fourteen hours in the clinical setting, six hours in faculty and committee meetings of the school, and some spend additional hours serving on university committees, four hours per week counseling students, eight hours preparing for class and clinical, eight hours grading student reports, quizzes, journals, and so on . . . two hours working with student teachers from the graduate program in nursing. In addition to this workload, faculty members are expected to be involved in community activities, pursue further formal education and conduct publishable research. All of the faculty members are involved in these latter activities to some extent, since the school's hiring, promotion and tenure policies place heavy emphasis upon them. Five faculty members are pursuing doctorates, four are conducting research and five are heavily involved in community or organized nursing activities.

The dean of the school is recognized as a leader in nursing and is most interested in establishing a reputation for the school. She sees this happening primarily through faculty research, publication and speaking. She also expects those faculty members without doctoral degrees to pursue them as rapidly as possible. The future viability of the school is dependent in large part upon accomplishment of these goals.

The clinical facilities available to the school consist of a small community nursing service, two 100-bed nursing homes and a 450-bed general hospital. The school has access to five units within the hospital which adequately meet the current clinical objectives of the program. The remaining units within the hospital are used by other nursing programs which affiliate at the facility. It is the general consensus of the faculty that both students and faculty are at best tolerated by the nursing staff on two of the units. How would you proceed in this situation if you were

   a. the concerned student group?
   b. the faculty group involved?
   c. the dean of this program?

CAUGHT BETWEEN A ROCK AND A HARD PLACE

Kathy Daley, a graduate with one and one-half years experience, who has been working on the unit for five months has been caring for Mrs. Thomas, a 52-year-old woman who recently had surgery for a colostomy. Mrs. Thomas has been recovering and has slowly begun to accept the change in body image resulting from the colostomy. Today, with a great deal of help from Kathy, she irrigated it for the first time. In the afternoon Dr. Marshal sees Mrs. Thomas and tells her she has recovered well and he will discharge her the next day. As an afterthought, he asks her if she has yet irrigated her colostomy, and upon hearing that she has, replies "good; then everything is set," and promptly disappears.

When Kathy returns from lunch, she hears from Mrs. Thomas that she is to be discharged the next day. Somewhat shocked, she asks Mrs. Thomas how she feels about this. Mrs. Thomas replies that it will be good to be home, but she is afraid that she won't be able to care for herself, nor will her 68-year-old sister with whom she lives. Kathy tells Mrs. Thomas that she will look into the situation. She approaches Jane Ward, the head nurse and asks her if she is aware that Mrs. Thomas is being discharged the next day. Miss Ward replies that she is and that Mrs. Thomas seems to be recovering quite nicely. Kathy then tells her of Mrs. Thomas's concerns and inability to adequately care for her colostomy. Miss Ward tells Kathy to allow her to irrigate it tomorrow and that should be adequate, replying "she will learn the rest at home." Kathy tells Miss Ward that she believes Mrs. Thomas needs a follow-up visit or two by the visiting nurse to assist her over the initial adjustment period at home. Miss Ward reminds Kathy that the doctor must order any follow-up visits of the community nursing service in this hospital.

"Why?" Kathy asks.

Miss Ward replies that although she personally doesn't agree with it, that's the way it's always been here. She reminds Kathy that it is a very conservative and traditional hospital where the doctor is considered head and calls all the moves.

"Well," replies Kathy, "I'll get in touch with Dr. Marshal and see what he says."

"I would prefer that you didn't," replies Miss Ward, "he is busy and doesn't like people suggesting how he should follow his patients. Something like this happened about two months ago, and he went into a rage, and relations on the unit were tolerable at best for sometime until he cooled down."

"Well, I can see the problem and can understand why we probably can't call Dr. Marshal, but what can we do about Mrs. Thomas?" asks Kathy.

"Don't worry about it," replies Jane, "she will be fine, you'll see."

How would you solve the immediate problem of meeting Mrs.

Thomas's needs without endangering your ability to deal with the larger problems in this situation?

YOUR TURN

In conclusion, you have now seen how individuals and groups have effected change in nursing. You have seen areas the authors, other nurses and hopefully you yourself believe need further change. You have reviewed change theory and have seen its application in specific situations.

The authors began from a premise that, for nurses to realize their full potential to make unique and valuable contributions to the creation of effective and humane systems of health care, they need both a theoretical grasp and practical skills for planning and directing change. This book will have partially satisfied that need. The remainder can be realized only as each of us reaches out to develop our own change skills.

The book was written as a statement of the possible. The nurses about whom we have just read made change possible in their situations. Why not you in yours? For those of you who are already using the change process successfully, a careful review of the summary results of the survey questionnaire will perhaps clarify areas needing further effort. For those of you who have not yet developed your change skills, now is the time! Begin by outlining your own frustrating situation:

Situation

Assessment
    Interest

    Motivation

Environment

Planning
Support Group

Goals

Sources of Power

Resistances

Strategies

Implementation

Evaluation

Stabilization

Appendix

As indicated in the preface, the responses of nurses to the authors' survey questionnaire provided the direction for sections of this book. The questionnaire, which identified major issues currently affecting nurses, was developed based on a survey of the nursing literature, issues raised during the authors' contacts with nursing colleagues and the authors' own experiences. The questions were designed so nurses might offer their opinions on issues in addition to responding to the authors' questions.

Eleven hundred questionnaires were sent to nurses working in a variety of settings randomly selected throughout the fifty states—urban hospitals, community hospitals, baccalaureate nursing programs, associate degree nursing programs and community health agencies. The questionnaires were mailed in mid-January of 1977 and the returns collated and analyzed in June 1977. Of the 1,100 questionnaires mailed, 362 were completed and returned, yielding a 32.9 percent response from a single mailing. From the total of 177 returns received from nurses in practice settings, 41 were from staff nurses, 15 from head nurses, 13 from clinical specialists and 108 from supervisors and administrators of nursing service. From the total of 185 returns received from nurses in educational settings, 72 were received from faculty in baccalaureate settings, 72 from faculty in associate degree settings and 41 from chairpersons or deans.

The responses were used to provide direction for Chapter Two, and the situations developed and analyzed in Chapter Four were chosen in response to the needs expressed by nurses who completed the survey. The following copy of the survey and analysis of the results are presented for review.

PLEASE ANSWER WHAT YOU BELIEVE—THERE IS NO "RIGHT" ANSWER

1. How can nurses demonstrate accountability for assuring quality patient (client) care?

The most common answers were (1) documentation of care given; (2) establishment of a plan of care with goals for each patient, revising the plan often and sticking with it; (3) use of primary nursing. Also (4) all of the mechanisms listed in question 2 were offered as answers to this question.

2. Which mechanism(s) do you feel should be used to ensure quality of patient (client) care? Check one or more.

77% Peer review
80% Outcome criteria (goals for patient care)
76% Nursing audit
42% Participation in PSROs
51% Mandatory continuing education

Comment:_____
_____
_____

3. If nursing is to have peer review:

   a. Who should review the performance of nurses? Check one or more.

52% Nurses working at peer level who are informed of the criteria for review
36% Nurses in supervisory positions
 7% Physicians
 4% Other health care professionals
    Other (specify) _____

Many nurses said they definitely did not want physicians to review the performance of nurses and felt very strongly about this issue.

b. Who should develop the criteria for review? Check one or more.

<u>47%</u> ANA
<u>36%</u> SNA
<u>34%</u> Consumers
<u>11%</u> Physicians
<u>74%</u> Nurses working in your agency
      Other (specify) *listed: nurse educators, NLN*

Comment:_____

_____

_____

4. Who should receive the results of peer evaluations?

By far the most common answer was the nurse being evaluated and her superior. Next was simply the nurse being evaluated. After these were nursing administration and hospital administration. A few nurses in each category—staff nurses, head nurses, supervisors, faculty, etc.—said that the results should be sent to the state board of nursing, the state nurses association, and/or the ANA.

5. As a result of peer evaluation, Nurse A receives an excellent rating; Nurse B, a satisfactory rating with a few recommendations for improvement; Nurse C, an extremely poor rating reflecting incompetence in practice. If you were to receive this information, what would you do with it?

This question drew general consensus. Respondents felt that Nurse A should be commended; many said she should have a merit raise and some suggested that she should be promoted. Nurse B, they felt, should have a meeting with her supervisor; she should be given suggestions and specific goals for improved performance. Nurse C should be placed on probation, be given less responsibility for a time and be assigned to attend appropriate inservice training; after a specified period she should be re-evaluated and, if no improvement has occurred, should be discharged. Several nurses cautioned that the results should be validated, to eliminate any possibility of personal bias, before action is taken. A few nurses suggested that Nurse C lose her license.

6. If nursing is to have outcome criteria, who should develop such criteria? Check one or more.

<u>78%</u> Nurses
<u>19%</u> Physicians
<u>15%</u> Other health disciplines
<u>36%</u> Consumers
<u>42%</u> Committee of all of the above.

7. Who do you think should be comparing the patient's (client's) progress with the established goals for the patient's (client's) care?

The highest numbers of responses were (1) nurses; (2) health team; (3) nurse and physician; (4) nurse and patient; (5) health team and patient; (6) nurse, physician, patient and family. Only a dozen nurses specified audit, audit committees or some formal peer review mechanism.

8. If the established goals for care are not realized due to negligence on the part of a team member or members, what should happen to:

a. The patient?
Response was almost unanimous that the patient should be informed of the failure to reach the goals. Most nurses felt that the patient should receive a new health team and/or nurse. Some said that the remainder of the patient's hospital stay should be free.

b. The negligent individual(s)?
Many respondents felt they lacked sufficient information to answer this question. Among those who answered, the general view was that the response should be related to whether the negligence was intentional; if it was based on lack of knowledge, they suggested that the individual be placed on probation and required to acquire the needed knowledge within a specified time.

9. If nurses are to participate in utilization review (Professional Services Review Organizations or PSROs), how can they function as consumer advocates in this role?

Forty percent had no response to this question. Those who did respond gave extremely varied answers. A few said that consumers should be their own advocates.

10. Do you feel a need to differentiate levels of performance for professional and technical (associate) nurses?

<u>62%</u> Yes
<u>16%</u> No
<u>5%</u> Don't know enough about subject

Comment:_____

_____

_____

11. Should there be different licensing examinations for professional and technical (associate) nurses?

<u>59%</u> Yes
<u>28%</u> No
<u>8%</u> Don't know

12. If there were different examinations, who do you feel should sit:

a. For the professional examination?
Of those who answered the question, two thirds said that BSNs should sit for the professional exam. Another one in ten would include diploma or ADN graduates with BSNs. It should be noted that a somewhat higher proportion of nurse educators responded to this question than did practicing nurses.

b. For the technical (associate) examination?
Of those who responded to this question, 44 percent felt that the technical exam should be for AD and diploma graduates; 27 percent specified AD only. Small numbers of respondents suggested including practical nurses.

13. Are you aware that certification for excellence in nursing practice is available in clinical specialties?

<u>87%</u> Yes
<u>10%</u> No

14. Who do you think should establish the criteria for certification for excellence in nursing practice? Check one or more.

<u>62%</u> ANA
<u>12%</u> Your own health care institution
<u>18%</u> State licensing bodies
<u>69%</u> Nurse specialty groups (e.g., American Assn. of Neurological Nurses)

___7%___ Physician specialty groups (e.g., American Academy of Pediatrics)

_____ Other (specify) _____

Comment: _____

_____

_____

Limit establishment of criteria to practicing nurses, NLN, NLN plus ANA, committee of all groups mentioned in question.

15. Do you feel a need for clarifying the role of the nurse as it relates to physicians and other allied health professionals?

___83%___ Yes
___15%___ No

Comment:_____

_____

_____

16. Do you see a need to provide consumers and the public with a more up-to-date image of the role and function of the nurse?

___91%___ Yes
___7%___ No

Comment:_____

_____

_____

17. Currently, do you feel nurses receive:

   a. Recognition for services provided?

___22%___ Yes
___65%___ No
___6%___ Don't know

   b. Salary commensurate with that of other professions with similar education, experience and job responsibility?

___17%___ Yes
___74%___ No
___5%___ Don't know

c. Opportunity for advancement commensurate with that enjoyed by other professionals?

<u>30%</u> Yes
<u>57%</u> No
<u> 9%</u> Don't know

d. Authority matching responsibility?

<u>19%</u> Yes
<u>70%</u> No
<u> 5%</u> Don't know

Comment:_____

_____

_____

18. Do you feel that nurses have adequate federal support for nursing research?

<u>17%</u> Yes
<u>60%</u> No

Comment: _____

_____

_____

Most common comment was don't know (15%). Many respondents commented that they perceived little interest, orientation, encouragement or support for research within the profession.

19. Do you feel that the Equal Rights Amendment would have a favorable impact on nursing?

<u>53%</u> Yes
<u>17%</u> No
<u>23%</u> Don't know enough about subject

Comment:_____

_____

_____

20. Do you feel the nursing profession should become more politically active? In what ways? Please explain. (Use extra sheet if needed.)

<u>68%</u> Yes;
<u>16%</u> No;
<u>16%</u> No answer.

The principal suggestions were lobbying for health legislation; becoming more active in nursing organizations (group political action); running for office and becoming directly involved in the political or public arena; changing nurse practice acts.

21. Do you believe that baccalaureate education should be the entry point into the profession of nursing?

<u>52%</u> Yes
<u>32%</u> No
<u>16%</u> Not certain

Comment:_____

_____

_____

22. Do you believe that the integrated, conceptually based baccalaureate nursing curricula advocated by the NLN have had/will have a positive impact on the quality of care delivered by professional nurses?

<u>29%</u> Yes
<u>10%</u> No
<u>29%</u> Too soon to tell
<u>27%</u> Don't know enough about subject

Comment:_____

_____

_____

23. How do you feel baccalaureate nursing education should be modified to reduce the "reality shock" phenomenon?

The most common response in all categories was more clinical experience for students. Other responses were (1) more realistic clinical experiences (working all three shifts, more than one or two patients); (2) internships after graduation; (3) instructors with ongoing clinical involvement; (4) initiation of nursing courses in freshman year.

24. Can the concept of "career ladder" work in professional nursing?

<u>62%</u> Yes
<u>12%</u> No
<u>19%</u> Don't know enough about subject

25. Is the external degree program a valid way to study professional nursing?

<u>20%</u> Yes
<u>32%</u> No
<u>40%</u> Don't know enough about subject

26. Studies show that recent nursing graduates are assuming roles for which they are not prepared. Do you agree? How would you like to see this problem resolved?

The response was almost unanimously "yes." The most commonly suggested solutions were (1) more clinical experience for students; (2) internships; (3) good inservice programs and orientation in employing institutions; (4) better staffing, so that new graduates don't have to assume too much responsibility and workload; (5) better communication between nursing service and nursing education. One respondent argued that employing institutions should set and enforce job standards that would prevent new graduates from assuming roles for which they're not prepared.

27. Do you feel that the present accreditation process makes nursing education accountable to:

a. Consumers of education (students)?

<u>47%</u> Yes
<u>21%</u> No
<u>28%</u> Not sure

b. Consumers of health care?

<u>31%</u> Yes
<u>27%</u> No
<u>34%</u> Not sure

Comment:_____

_____

_____

28. Should the accreditation process be continued?

90% Yes
_3% No

If not, how do you feel we should ensure quality control in nursing education?

29. Should continuing education be mandatory for renewal of licensure?

67% Yes
29% No

Comment: _____

_____
_____

Four percent were not sure or did not answer. Nurses in every category expressed concern about who would pay for continuing education if it were mandatory.

30. Do you feel that dual appointments would improve communication between nursing education and service?

58% Yes
13% No
29% Don't know

Comment:_____

_____
_____

31. In the financing of nursing education:

a. Do you believe that the criteria for capitation grants should be changed?

27% Yes
_7% No
66% Don't know enough about subject

b. Should federal funding be contingent on mandatory service in "underserved" areas?

27% Yes
40% No
33% Don't know enough about subject

c. Do you believe that regional planning would provide for more effective use of money and resources in nursing education?

63% Yes
_7% No
30% Don't know enough about subject

Comment on changes you would like to see in funding for nurse education: _____

_____

_____

32. What do you feel is the role of the doctorally prepared nurse within the profession? Within the health care delivery system?

Most respondents identified a research role (46%), an educational role (41%), an administrative role (16%) and a role in clinical practice (10%)

33. Are there any other areas of nursing in which you feel there is a need for change?
a. In nursing education?
In all categories of nursing service and among AD and BSN faculty, need was clearly expressed for more clinical experience in student's education; however, none of the educational program chairpersons or deans expressed such a need. The only other answers given by ten or more respondents were (1) more qualified teachers; this answer was given in general terms or in terms of specific qualifications, such as clinical involvement; and (2) placing all nursing education in instititutions of higher learning.
b. In nursing practice?
The most common responses centered around (1) less paperwork; (2) more direct patient care; and (3) greater professional autonomy. Beyond these, there were numerous and varied responses covering many aspects of nursing organization, quality assurance, staff-patient ratios, continuing education, pay and so on.
c. In nursing administration?
The most frequent responses here were (1) requirement of ad-

vanced nursing degree in administrative roles; (2) need for more voice of nursing administration in policy making; (3) better communication between administration and staff, and (4) more clinical skills for administrators.

34. Is there any situation with which you come into contact in your daily work that you would like to change but have been unable to? Please describe.

The most commonly identified situations were developed and analyzed in Chapter Four. The following situations were also frequently identified as requiring change: need for (1) increased salaries; (2) increased sense of self-worth; (3) increased involvement and support for research and writing; (4) increased autonomy of the nursing role; (5) increased communication and cooperation between health care professionals; (6) need to consider experiential background and past performance in addition to educational background in appointment and promotion; (7) acceptance as peers by physicians; (8) need to be more supportive of each other; (9) increased availability of advanced programs for RNs and masters programs; (10) increased political involvement; (11) need to function more accountably.

The authors would like to thank all of the individuals who responded to our survey questionnaire. Many individual nurses not only returned the questionnaire but expressed willingness to have their views on issues quoted or referenced. These included nurses working in the following institutions and agencies, which are listed to give some idea of the variety and geographical distribution of the settings within which the survey respondents worked. Appearance on this list is not intended to imply that the institution or agency has endorsed either the responses of its individual faculty or staff members or the survey results as a whole.

Baptist Medical Center-Montclair, Birmingham, Ala.

Jefferson County Department of Health, Birmingham, Ala.

Bartlett Memorial Hospital, Juneau, Alaska

University of Alaska, Anchorage

University of Arizona, Tucson

St. Vincent Infirmary, Little Rock, Ark.

University of Central Arkansas, Convoy

University of California-San Francisco

University of Northern Colorado, Greeley

Nursing Section, Colorado Department of Health, Denver

Rockville Public Health Nursing Association, Rockville, Conn.

Beebe Hospital, Lewes, Del.

Wesley College, Dover, Del.

American University, Washington, D.C.

James M. Jackson Memorial Hospital, Miami, Fla.

Florida A & M University, Tallahassee

157

Valencia Community College, Orlando, Fla.

Medical Center of Central Georgia, Macon

Memorial Hospital, Bainbridge, Ga.

Georgia State University, Atlanta

Queen's Medical Center, Honolulu, Hawaii

University of Hawaii, Honolulu

Honolulu Home Care Service, St. Francis Hospital, Honolulu

St. Luke's Hospital, Boise, Idaho

Ricks College, Rexburg, Idaho

Southwest District Health Department, Boise, Idaho

Indiana University-Purdue University at Fort Wayne

St. Joseph Mercy Hospital, Sioux City, Iowa

Mahaska County Hospital, Oskaloosa, Iowa

Iowa Wesleyan College, Mt. Pleasant

Public Health Nurses' Association of Linn County, Cedar Rapids, Iowa

Marymount College, Salina, Kans.

Hesston College, Hesston, Kans.

Topeka-Shawnee County Health Department, Kans.

King's Daughter's Hospital, Shelbyville, Ky.

Louisiana State University, New Orleans

Northwestern State University of Louisiana, Shreveport

University of Maine, Augusta

University of Maine, Portland

Anne Arundel Community College, Arnold, Md.

Instructive Visiting Nurse Association of Baltimore City, Md.

Massachusetts General Hospital, Boston

Boston College, Chestnut Hill, Mass.

Visiting Nurse Association, Worcester, Mass.

Blodgett Memorial Medical Center, Grand Rapids, Mich.

Lansing Community College, Lansing, Mich.

Visiting Nurse Association of Saginaw, Mich.

College of St. Scholastica, Duluth, Minn.

Rochester State Community College, Rochester, Minn.

University of Missouri, Columbia

William Jewell College, Kansas City, Mo.

Montana Deaconess Hospital, Great Falls

Northern Montana College, Havre

Creighton University, Omaha, Neb.

University of Nebraska, Omaha

University of Nevada, Las Vegas

Western Nevada Community College, Reno

St. Anselm's College, Manchester, N.H.

Visiting Nurse Association of Manchester, N.H., Inc.

State University-Rutgers, Newark, N.J.

Presbyterian Hospital, Albuquerque, N.Mex.

Junior College of Albany, New York

Onslow Memorial Hospital, Jacksonville, N.C.

Duke University, Durham, N.C.

Rockingham Community College, Wentworth, N.C.

Trinity Medical Center, Minot, N.D.

Mercy Hospital, Valley City, N.D.

Good Samaritan Hospital, Cincinnati, Ohio

Blackwell General Hospital, Blackwell, Okla.

University of Tulsa, Okla.

Bacone College, Muskogee, Okla.

St. Elizabeth Community Hospital, Baker, Ore.

University of Oregon, Portland

Chemeketa Community College, Salem, Ore.

Children's Hospital of Pittsburgh, Pa.

Bucks County Community College, Newtown, Pa.

University of Rhode Island, Kingston

Rhode Island Junior College, Providence

Newberry County Memorial Hospital, Newberry, S.C.

Clemson University, Clemson, S.C.

Appalachia III Public Health District Nursing Services, Spartanburg, S.C.

Mobridge Community Hospital, Mobridge, S.D.

Presentation College, Aberdeen, S.D.

University of Tennessee, Memphis

Motlow State Community College, Tullahoma, Tenn.

Chattanooga-Hamilton County Health Department, Tenn.

Seymour Hospital Authority, Seymour, Texas

Texas Christian University-Harris College of Nursing, Forth Worth

Lamar University, Beaumont, Texas

University of Utah Medical Center, Salt Lake City

Weber State College, Ogden, Utah

Medical Center of Vermont, Burlington

Castleton State College, Castleton, Vt.

Medical College of Virginia, Richmond

University of Virginia, Charlottesville

Virginia Western Community College, Roanoke

Instructive Visiting Nurse Association, Richmond, Va.

Tacoma General Hospital, Tacoma, Wash.

Seattle-King County Visiting Nurse Service, Wash.

Charleston Area Medical Center, Charleston, W.Va.

West Virginia University, Morgantown

Marshall University, Huntington, W.Va.

Memorial Medical Center, Ashland, Wis.

University of Wisconsin, Eau Claire

Wausau Visiting Nurse Association, Wausau, Wis.

Memorial Hospital of Natrona County, Casper, Wyo.

Casper College, Casper, Wyo.

Wyoming Division of Health & Medical Services, Cheyenne

Bibliography

CHAPTER ONE

Benedikter, Helen. *The Nursing Audit . . . . a Necessity. How Shall It Be Done?* New York: National League for Nursing, 1973.

Bullough, Bonnie and Bullough, Vern. *The Emergence of Modern Nursing.* New York: The Macmillan Company, 1969.

Cleland, Virginia. "The Professional Model." *American Journal of Nursing* 75:288–292, February 1975.

Cook, Sir Edward. *The Life of Florence Nightingale.* New York: The Macmillan Company, 1942.

Cope, Zachary. *Florence Nightingale and The Doctors.* Philadelphia: J. B. Lippincott Company, 1958.

Coulton, Mary R. "Labor Disputes: A Challenge to Nurse Staffing." *Journal of Nursing Administration* 15–20, May 1976.

Creighton, Helen (ed.). "Current Legal and Professional Issues." *Nursing Clinics of North America.* Philadelphia: W. B. Saunders Company, September 1974.

Dock, Lavinia L. "Lavinia L. Dock—Self Portrait." *Nursing Outlook* 25:22–26, January 1977.

Douglas, Emily Taft. *Pioneer of the Future—Margaret Sanger.* New York: Holt, Rinehart and Winston, 1970.

Driscoll, Veronica M. "The Myth of Two Hats." *The Journal of the New York State Nurses Association* 4(4):36–39, November 1973.

Ford, Loretta and Kohnke, Mary. "The Nurse Practitioner Question." *American Journal of Nursing* 74:2188–2191, December 1974.

Heneman, Herbert G. Jr. "Collective Bargaining a Major Instrument for Change." *American Journal of Nursing* 68:1039–1042, May 1968.

Herzog, Thomas P. "The National Labor Relations Act and the ANA: A Dilemma of Professionalism." *Journal of Nursing Administration* 34–36, October 1976.

Jacox, Ada. "Collective Bargaining in Academe: Background and Perspective." *Nursing Outlook* 21(11):700–703, November 1973.

Jensen, Deborah. *History and Trends of Professional Nursing*. St. Louis: The C.V. Mosby Company, 1950.

Kalisch, Beatrice and Kalisch, Philip A. "Slaves, Servants, or Saints?" *Nursing Forum* 11(3):223–263, 1975.

Kennedy, David M. *Birth Control in America—The Career of Margaret Sanger*. New Haven: Yale University Press, 1970.

Lysaught, Jerome P. *Action in Nursing Progress in Professional Purpose*. New York: McGraw-Hill Book Company, 1974.

Miller, Michael H. "Nurses' Right to Strike." *Journal of Nursing Administration* 35–39, February 1975.

———. "PSROs—Boon or Bust for Nursing?" *Hospitals* 49:81–84, October 1, 1975.

Munson, Helen W. *The Story of the National League of Nursing Education*. Philadelphia: W. B. Saunders Company, 1934.

Nash, Rosalind. *A Short Life of Florence Nightingale*. New York: The Macmillan Company, 1925.

National League for Nursing. *Accountability the Obligation of the Educational Institution to the Consumer*. New York: National League for Nursing, 1977.

———. *Regulatory Agencies—The Effect on Health Care Institutions*. New York: National League for Nursing, 1974.

O'Malley, I. B. *Florence Nightingale 1820–1856*. London: Thornton Butterworth, Limited, 1931.

Palmer, Irene S. "Florence Nightingale: Reformer, Reactionary, Researcher." *Nursing Research* 29:84–89, March–April 1977.

Pennock, Meta. *Makers of Nursing History*. New York: Lakeside Publishing, 1940.

Robinson, Victor. *White Caps—The Story of Nursing*. Philadelphia: J. B. Lippincott Company. 1946.

Stahl, Adele. "State Boards of Nursing: Legal Aspects." *Nursing Clinics of North America* 505–572, September 1971.

Tescher, Barbara E. and Colavecchio, Ruth. "Definition of a Standard for Clinical Nursing Practice." *Journal of Nursing Administration* 32–44, March 1977.

Yost, Edna. *American Women of Nursing*. Philadelphia: J. B. Lippincott Company, 1955.

Zimmerman, Anne. "ANA Its Record on Social Issues." *American Journal of Nursing* 76:588–590, April 1976.

CHAPTER TWO

Ashley, J. "About Power in Nursing." *Nursing Outlook* 21:637–641, 1973.

Bentley, Peter. *Health Care Agencies and Professionals: A Changing Relationship.* New York: National League for Nursing, 1977.

Bernal, H. "Power and Interorganizational Health Care Projects." *Nursing Outlook* 24:419–421, 1976.

Bindler, Ruth. "Moral Development in Nursing Education." *Image* 9:18–20, February 1977.

Brazil, Ann. "An Inspiration for All New Graduates." *Nursing Digest* 53, November–December 1975.

Chapoorian, Teresa and Craig, Margaret M. "PL93-641-Nursing and Health Care Delivery." *American Journal of Nursing* 76:1988–1991, December 1976.

Damico, Sancha and Nevill, Dorothy. "Developmental Components of Role Conflict in Women." *The Journal of Psychology* 195–198, 1977.

Deloughery, G. L. and Gebbie, K. M. *Political Dynamics: Impact on Nurses and Nursing.* St. Louis: The C. V. Mosby Company, 1975.

Downs, Florence S. "Technological Advance and the Nurse-Family Relationship." *Nursing Digest* 22–24, May–June 1975.

Estok, Patricia J. "Socialization Theory and Entry into the Practice of Nursing." *Image* 9:8–14, February 1977.

Fagin, Claire M. "Nurses' Rights." *American Journal of Nursing* 75:82–85, January 1975.

Fahy, Ellen T. "A Battery of Techniques for Dodging Issues." *Image* 9:21–22, February 1977.

Fine, Ruth B. "Nursing Educators, Nursing Directors: A Symbiotic Relationship." *Nurse Educator* 1:4–7, September–October 1976.

Haase, Patricia T. "Pathways to Practice-Part I." *American Journal of Nursing* 76:806–809, May 1976.

Hayman, Howard S. "Models of Human Nature and Their Impact on Health Education." *Nursing Digest* 37–40, September–October 1975.

Heiman, C. G. "Four Theories of Leadership." *Journal of Nursing Administration* 6(5):18–28, 1976.

Hyde, Ann. "The Phenomenon of Caring." *American Nurses Foundation— Nursing Research Report* 11:12–15, February 1976.

Jackson, Bettie S. "Will the Nursing Profession Survive? Graduate Students Debate the Issues." *Nurse Educator* 7–9, January–February 1977.

Kaiser, Barbara L. and Irwin H. "The Challenge of the Women's Movement to American Gynecology." *Nursing Digest* 23–25, January–February 1976.

Kalisch, Beatrice J. and Kalisch, Philip A. "A Discourse on the Politics of Nursing." *Journal of Nursing Administration* 29–34, 1976.

Kaye, D. "The Woman Boss: Getting There Is Only Half the Problem." *Mainliner* 20(6):34–37, 1976.

Kellams, Samuel E. "Ideals of a Profession: The Case of Nursing." *Image* 9:30–31, June 1977.

Kirschenbaum, Howard; Howe, Leland W. and Simon, Sidney B. *Values Clarification*. New York: Hart Publishing Company Inc., 1972.

Kramer, Marlene and Schmalenberg, Claudia E. "Conflict: The Cutting Edge of Growth." *Journal of Nursing Administration* 19–25, October 1976.

Lewis, Howard L. "Wave of Union Organizing Will Follow Break in the Taft-Hartley Dam." *Nursing Digest* 60–62, May–June 1975.

Loring, R., and Wells, T. *Breakthrough: Women into Management*. New York: Van Nostrand Reinhold Company, 1972.

MacPhail, Jannetta. "Promoting Collaboration Between Education and Service." *Nurse Educator* 1:19–21, September–October 1976.

Mayo, Ross P. "A Nurse Can Be a Man or a Woman." *American Journal of Nursing* 77:1318–1319, August 1976.

McBride, Angela B. "A Married Feminist." *American Journal of Nursing* 76:754–757, May 1976.

McGriff, Erline P. "The Courage for Effective Leadership in Nursing." *Image* 8:56–60, October 1976.

Mullane, Mary K. "Nursing Care and the Political Arena." *Nursing Outlook* 669–701, November 1975.

National League for Nursing. *Accountability—Accepting The Challenge*. New York: National League for Nursing, 1976.

———. *Collaboration Between Service and Education: Fact or Fancy*. New York: National League for Nursing, 1971.

———. *Collaboration for Quality Health Care*. New York: National League for Nursing, 1977.

———. *Conflict Management—Flight, Fight, Negotiate?* New York: National League for Nursing, 1977.

———. *People Power*. New York: National League for Nursing, 1976.

———. *People Power—Politics for Health Care*. New York: National League for Nursing, 1976.

———. *Perspectives for Nursing*. New York: National League for Nursing, June 1975.

———. *Productivity*. New York: National League for Nursing, 1977.

———. *The Issue Is Leadership*. New York: National League for Nursing, 1975.

Nolan, M. G. "Wanted: Colleagueship in Nursing." *Journal of Nursing Administration* 6(3):41–43, 1976.

Novello, Dorothy. "The National Health Planning and Resources Development Act." *Nursing Outlook* 354–358, June 1976.

Osborne, Oliver H. "Issues in Achieving Effective Professional Alliances." *Nursing Digest* 56–59, January–February 1976.

Phillips, John R. "Nursing Systems and Nursing Models." *Image* 9:4–7, February 1977.

Powers, Marjorie J. "The Unification Model in Nursing." *Nursing Outlook* 482–487, August 1976.

Rosenberg, Stanley and Judkins, Beatrice. "Federal Programs Make Education an Integral Part of Patient Care." *Hospitals* 62 May 1, 1976.

Schlotfeldt, R. "On the Professional Status of Nursing." *Nursing Forum* XIII(1):17–31, 1974.

Schmidt, Susan M. "Using a Student Run Community Agency for Clinical Experience." *Nurse Educator* 16–21, May–June 1977.

Sills, Grayce M. "Nursing, Medicine and Hospital Administration." *American Journal of Nursing* 76:1432–1434, September 1976.

Simms, Elsie. "Preparation for Independent Practice." *Nursing Outlook* 25:114–118, February 1977.

Stafford, Linda L. "Scape Goating." *American Journal of Nursing* 77:406–408, March 1977.

Steckel, Susan B. "Utilization of Reinforcement Contracts to Increase Written Evidence of the Nursing Assessment." *Nursing Research* 25:58–61, January–February 1976.

Stevenson, Joanne S. "Guest Editorial–Nursing Research and the Industrial Community." *Image* 9:3, February 1977.

Stromborg, Marilyn F. "Relationship of Sex Role Identity to Occupational Image of Female Nursing Students." *Nursing Research* 25:363–369, September–October 1976.

Styles, Margretta and Gottdank, Mildred. "Nursing Vulnerability." *American Journal of Nursing* 76:1978–1980, December 1976.

The Robert Wood Johnson Foundation. "Nurse Practitioners Accent Care in Rural Family Practices." *The Report Wood Johnson Foundation Special Report* 2–5, February 1977.

Thomstad, Beatrice; Cunningham, Nicholas and Kaplan, Barbara. "Changing the Rules of the Doctor-Nurse Game." *Nursing Outlook* 422–427, July 1975.

Tobin, Helen, M.; Wengerd, Judy S. and Wykle, May H. "Leadership Development at the Clinical Unit Level." *Nursing Digest* 45–50, May–June 1975.

Uustal, Diane B. "Searching for Values." *Image* 9:15–17, February 1977.

Wachter-Shikora, Nancy. "Scapegoating Among Professionals." *American Journal of Nursing* 77:408–409, March 1977.

Wang, Rosemary and Watson, Joellen. "Laws on Sex Discrimination and Their Implications for Women in Higher Education." *Image* 8:52–56, October 1976.

CHAPTER THREE

Alpander, G. and Gutmann, J. "A Model for Measuring the Impact of Change on an Organization." *Hospital and Community Psychiatry* 25:719–723, November 1974.

Altman, I. *The Environment and Social Behavior.* Monterey, California: Brooks/Cole Publishing Company, 1975.

Aspree, Elsie. "The Process of Change." *Supervisor Nurse* 6:15–24, October 1975.

Bailey, J. T. and Claus, K. E. *Decision Making in Nursing: Tools for Change.* St. Louis: The C. V. Mosby Company, 1975.

Beletz, Elaine E. and Meng, Mary T. "The Grievance Process." *American Journal of Nursing* 77:256–260, February 1977.

Berkowitz, Norman and Malone, Mary. "Intra-Professional Conflict." *Nursing Forum* 7(1):51–71, 1968.

Brouwer, P. J. "The Power to See Ourselves." *Harvard Business Review* 54(1):66–73, 1976.

Copp, Laurel Archer. "Inservice Education Copes with Resistance to Change." *Journal of Continuing Education in Nursing* 6(2):19–27, March–April 1975.

Craig, J. H. and Craig, M. *Synergic Power: Beyond Domination and Permissiveness.* Berkeley, California: Pro Active Press, 1974.

Day, Harvey. "Change Can Be Planned and Effected." *Supervisor Nurse* 47–49, March 1974.

Dornbusch, S. M. and Scott W. R. *Evaluation and the Exercise of Authority.* San Francisco: Jossey-Bass Inc. Publishers, 1975.

Driscoll, V. M. "Independence in Nursing: Challenge or Burden? Can We Exist Without It?" *Michigan Nurse* 45:12–15, 1972.

Dyer, W. G. *The Sensitive Manipulator.* Provo, Utah: Brigham Young University Press, 1972.

Felker, D. W. *Building Positive Self Concepts.* Minneapolis: Burgess Publishing Company, 1974.

Fidler, F. E. and Chemers, M. *Leadership and Effective Management.* Glenview, Illinois: Scott, Foresman and Company, 1974.

Hersey, Paul and Blanchard, Kenneth H. *Management of Organizational Behavior* (2nd ed.). Englewood Cliffs, New Jersey: Prentice-Hall, Inc., 1972.

Herzberg, Frederick. *Work and the Nature of Man.* Ohio: World Book, 1969.

Insel, P. and Moos, R. *The Work Environment Scale.* Palo Alto, California: Stanford University Social Ecology Laboratory, Department of Psychiatry, 1972.

Johnson, D. W. *The Constructive Use of Conflict.* In Johnson, D. W. *Contemporary Social Psychology.* Philadelphia: J. B. Lippincott Company, 1973.

Kipnis, D. and Vanderveer, B. "Ingratiation and the Use of Power." *Journal of Personality and Social Psychology* 17:280–286, 1971.

Lawrence, Paul. "How to Deal with Resistance to Change." *Harvard Business Review* Vol. 47:4–8, 166–176, January–February 1969.

Lee, Irene. "Cope with Resistance to Change." *Nursing '73* 6–7 March 1973.

Levenstein, Aaron. "Problem-solving Techniques for Managing Change." *Hospital Topics* 52:42, September–October 1974.

Lewis, E. P. "Accountability: How, for What, and to Whom?" *Nursing Outlook* 20(5):315, 1972.

Lindskold, S. and Tedeschi, J. T. "Reward Power and Attraction in Interpersonal Conflict." *Psychonomic Science* 22:211–213, 1971.

McClelland, D. "The Two Faces of Power." In Kolb, D. A.; Rubin, I. M.

and McIntyre, J. M. (eds.). *Organizational Psychology: A Book of Readings.* Englewood Cliffs, New Jersey: Prentice-Hall, Inc., 1974.

McClelland, D. and Burham, D. "Power Is the Great Motivator." *Harvard Business Review* 54(2):100–110, 1976.

McCloskey, J. "High Staff Nurse Turnover Rate Attributed to Low Self Esteem." *OR Reporter* 9:3, 1974.

McMullan, D. "Accountability and Nursing Education." *Nursing Outlook* 23(8):501–503, 1975.

Meininger, J. *Success Through Transactional Analysis.* New York: New American Library, Inc. (Signet Books), 1973.

Millard, R. M. "The New Accountability." *Nursing Outlook* 23(8):496–500, 1975.

Mullane, M. K. "Nursing Care and the Political Arena." *Nursing Outlook* 23(11):699–701, 1975.

Pierce, S. F., et al. "Changing Practice: By Choice Rather Than Chance." *Journal of Nursing Administration* 6:33–39, February 1976.

Pollard, W. E. and Mitchell T. R. "Decision Theory Analysis of Social Power." *Psychological Bulletin* 78(6):433–446, 1972.

Pym, B. "The Making of a Successful Pressure Group." *British Journal of Sociology* 24(4):448–461, 1973.

Reiff, R. "The Control of Knowledge: The Power of the Helping Professions." *Journal of Applied Behavioral Science* 10:451–461, 1974.

Reinkemeyer, Agnes M. "Nursing's Need Commitment to an Ideology of Change." *Nursing Forum* 9(4):340–355, 1970.

Ringer, R. J. *Winning Through Intimidation.* Los Angeles: Los Angeles Book Publishers Company, 1974.

Rodgers, J. "The Clinical Specialist as a Change Agent." *Journal of Psychiatric Nursing* 12:5–9, November–December 1974.

Rodgers, J. "Theoretical Considerations Involved in the Process of Change." *Nursing Forum* 13(2):160–174, 1973.

Rubin, I. and Beckhard, R. "Factors Influencing the Effectiveness of Health Teams." *Milbank Quarterly* 50(3):317–1972.

Sampson, R. V. *The Psychology of Power.* New York: Pantheon Books, Inc., 1965.

Stevens, Barbara. "Effecting Change." *Journal of Nursing Administration* 23–26, February 1975.

Tedeschi, J. T. (ed.). *The Social Influence Process.* Chicago: Aldine Publishing Company, 1972.

Walton, R. "Quality of Working Life: What Is It?" *Sloan Management Review* 15:11–23, 1973.

Wood, M. T. "Power Relationships and Group Decision Making in Organizations." *Psychological Bulletin* 79(5):280–293, 1973.

Index